F R O N T
O F F I C E
OPERATIONS
and
N I G H T
A U D I T
WORKBOOK

FRONT OFFICE OPERATIONS
and
NIGHT AUDIT WORKBOOK

Patrick J. Moreo
New Mexico State University

Gail Sammons
Oklahoma State University

Jim Dougan
University of Missouri

PRENTICE HALL, Upper Saddle River, NJ 07458

Director of Production and Manufacturing: *Bruce Johnson*
Managing Editor: *Mary Carnis*
Acquisitions Editor: *Neil Marquardt*
Manufacturing Buyer: *Ed O'Dougherty*
Editorial/production supervision : *Carol Lavis*
Marketing Manager: *Frank Mortimer, Jr.*
Cover design: *Bruce Kenselaar*

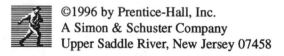

©1996 by Prentice-Hall, Inc.
A Simon & Schuster Company
Upper Saddle River, New Jersey 07458

Printed in the United States of America

10 9 8 7 6 5 4 3 2 1

ISBN 0-13-398769-8

Prentice-Hall International (UK) Limited, *London*
Prentice-Hall of Australia Pty. Limited, *Sydney*
Prentice-Hall Canada Inc., *Toronto*
Prentice-Hall Hispanoamericana, S.A., *Mexico*
Prentice-Hall of India Private Limited, *New Delhi*
Prentice-Hall of Japan, Inc., *Tokyo*
Simon & Schuster Asia Pte. Ltd., *Singapore*
Editora Prentice-Hall do Brasil, Ltda., *Rio de Janeiro*

Contents

Introduction ix

Preface x

Notes to Instructors xi

Notes to Students xii

Manual Night Audit Instructions and Exercises 1

Section 1 2

The Night Audit of Accounts Receivable 2

Section 2 4

Night Audit Formula 4

Section 3 6

Directions for the Student Exercise 6

Section 4 7

Sample Job Analysis for the Manual Night Audit 7

Section 5 8

Sample Night Audit Exercise for the University Inn 8
    Introduction 8
    Sample Exercise 8
    Sample Registration Card 13
    Sample Folio 15
    Sample Control Sheets 17
    Sample Vouchers 19
    Sample Front Office Cash Sheet 21
    Sample Cash Turn-in Envelope and Closing Bank Count 23
    Sample Room and House Count 25
    Sample Daily Transcript 27

Section 6 28

Night Audit Exercise for the University Inn - Problem Set No. I 28
     Introduction 28
     Exercise 28

Section 7 32

Night Audit Exercise for the University Inn - Problem Set No. II 32
     Introduction 32
     Exercise 32

Section 8 36

Night Audit Exercise for the University Inn - Problem Set No. III 36
     Introduction 36
     Exercise 36

Manual Night Audit Forms 41
     Registration Cards 41
     Folios 61
     Restaurant and Beverage Department Control Sheets 111
     Long Distance and Local Telephone Control Sheets 119
     Allowance and Laundry Department Control Sheets 127
     Credit Vouchers 135
     Charge Vouchers 165
     Front Office Cash Sheet 195
     Cash Turn-in Envelope and Closing Bank Count 207
     Room and House Count Sheet 219
     Daily Transcript Sheet 231

InnSyst - Front Desk Simulation Instructions and Exercise 243

Section 1 244

Introduction 244
     System Requirements 244

Section 2 245

Installation and Start-up 245
     Hard Disk Installation 245
     Removing Software from Hard Disk 245

Start-Up and Initialization 246
     Figure 2.1: Initialization Screen 246

Section 3 247

The Front Office Exercise 247
    Introduction 247
    Exercise 247
        Front Desk Transactions (11/14/95) 247
        Reports 249
        Cash on hand 250

Section 4 251

The Front Desk Main Menu 251
     Figure 4.1: The Front Desk Main Menu 251

Section 5 252

Front Desk Operations 252
    A.   Check-in 252
        Figure 5.1: Registration Entry Screen 252
    B.   Charge Posting 254
        Figure 5.2: Charge Posting Screen 254
    C.   Credit Posting 255
    D.   Edit Guest 256
    E.   Correct Credits 256
    F.   Change Rooms 256
    G.   View Folio 256
    H.   Check-out 257
    I.   Late Charges 257

Section 6 258

Night Audit and Utilities 258
    A.   Room Charges 258
    B.   Re-index Files 258
    C.   End of Day 259

Section 7 260
    Reports 260

InnSyst Sample Reports 262

University Inn
      Transaction Report for 11/14/95 263

University Inn
      Ledger Report for 11/14/95 264

University Inn
      D Card Report for 11/14/95 265

University Inn
      Statistics Report for 11/14/95 266

University Inn
      Daily Cash Reportfor 11/14/95 267

Cash Turn-in Envelope for InnSyst Night Audit Exercise 269

Notes 273

Introduction

The goal of the *Workbook* exercises is to provide the user with a clearer insight into front office and guest accounting and operations. We accomplish this by having the student begin by performing a simple, manual audit of the guest accounts receivable, and then conclude with a computerized version of accomplishing the same thing.

While there are some hotels and inns which continue to use a hand transcript, the purpose here is not to necessarily teach the student "how to" perform the manual night audit. Rather, we hope that the insight gained by seeing all the components of the night audit laid out before them would provide the users with the basic tools necessary to transfer their understanding to all other electronic and computer systems developed for performing the front office accounting function. These systems all change very rapidly in technical respects, but the underlying theories and principles remain the same: an audit and reconciliation of guests' bills with pertinent hotel records through standard bookkeeping and accounting techniques.

This edition, now entitled *Front Office Operations and Night Audit Workbook* recognizes that the title *Night Audit Workbook* needed to be more descriptive. The student actually performs an entire day's front office transactions before beginning the audit itself. The preliminary front office guest management part exercise should put front office accounting operations into cycled perspective. For this reason, we strongly urge the student to complete each problem in the order in which the components of that problem appear--as though they were working in the front office from the morning on through the day and evening shifts and finally ending with the night audit itself.

The "computer" section of this book is designed to flow from the manual foundation which we have laid. The goal is for the student to understand, that regardless of the techniques used, ultimately it is a clear *system* design which will lead to the goal of providing the guest with excellent, quick service and the hotel with accurate records. The student should have a clear understanding that indeed, with evolving computer driven systems, many of the checks and balances in the original manual system become unnecessary because the possibility for posting error, for example, is eliminated. The *Workbook* reinforces theory with practice.

Preface

This *Workbook* is the result of experimentation in Front Office operations classes at the University of Nevada, Las Vegas over a twelve year period, The Pennsylvania State University for seven years, and New Mexico State and Oklahoma State Universities for one year. The exercise is intended as a reinforcement for the guest/room management as well as the accounting and night audit--"close of day" sections of lectures and textbooks in front office or hotel operations courses.

The *Front Office Operations and Night Audit Workbook* design is compatible with the corresponding sections of the major front office texts in use and under development. It will reinforce those sections of the texts with practical exercises.

The concept of using a practice set to reinforce classroom instruction is not new. As students at the then New York City Community College in the mid-1960's, we used similar approaches under the direction of Professor Sam Iseman. I would like to remember the late Sam Iseman for his dedication and inspiration.

This fourth edition is new in many ways. I am very fortunate to have two new partners in this endeavor. Mr. Jim Dougan designed and wrote the entire computer section and the *InnSyst* part of the exercise. He spent many hours working on this most detailed task and several semesters testing the process and the software in the classroom.

Dr. Gail Sammons wrote the new Problem Set III. It is designed to be a stand alone problem which instructors can use for further reinforcement. In addition, she updated and re-designed the forms which we use in the book. Gail also took on the responsibility of managing the compilation of the final text.

I received comments and suggestions from other instructors who have used this book and incorporated them into this edition. Please continue to communicate them to any of us.

Patrick J. Moreo, Ed.D., CHA
Las Cruces, New Mexico
April, 1996

Notes to Instructors

* Enough forms are included for two of the three manual problem sets contained in this workbook. Problem sets I and II are sequential, while Problem set III is unrelated to the other two.

* We have found it quite beneficial to change one or two numbers for each class so that some of the final figures will be different from semester to semester. This is relatively simple to do especially if you change those figures which will not affect the cash totals. If you contact me I can provide you with further details on implementing this system with a minimum of effort.

   Also available now, is a diskette for instructors which has the solution sets on it and which can also be used to generate slight differences in the problem sets themselves. This helps in making certain that each semester and each section is challenged problem sets which are uniquely theirs.

* You can request hard copy solution sets or diskettes by contacting your Prentice Hall representative. Or you may contact any of us directly for information:

   Dr. Patrick J. Moreo
   Hospitality and Tourism Management
   College of Agriculture and Home Economics
   New Mexico State University
   P.O. Box 30003, Dept. 3HTS
   Las Cruces, New Mexico   88003-0003

   Dr. Gail Sammons
   Department of Hotel Management
   William F Harrah College of Hotel Administration
   University of Nevada Las Vegas
   Box 456021   4505 Maryland Parkway
   Las Vegas, Nevada 89154-6021

   Mr. Jim Dougan
   Assistant Professor
   Food Science & Human Nutrition
   122 Eckles Hall
   Columbia, MO 65211

Notes to Students

①   This workbook is designed to help you understand the basics of designing and operating a system of guest accounts receivable in the front office of a hotel or other lodging facility. It has been our experience and our belief, after teaching hundreds of students and conducting discussions with alumni in the years after they have graduated, that an understanding of the "manual" system is crucial to the comprehension of other systems.

Use of this manual system will make it very easy for you to see each component of the front office accounting system and how that component is interrelated to all of the other parts of the system. The reason for this is that you will actually be manipulating each of these parts yourself.

②   With this basic understanding, future application of the knowledge gained makes a lot more sense. So, when you begin to learn about the various electronic systems available or about the plethora of computer systems, you will know what these systems are supposed to do--because you have done it yourself!

Indeed, you will then be able to clearly see what it is you would like the computer programs to do, and what is no longer necessary compared to the manual or electronic systems. The perfect follow up to performing these manual exercises is to do the same thing using a computer front office or property management system such as H.I.S., Lodgistix, Fidelio or any number of fine software packages available either at your next job, or in a computer laboratory that you might have available in your school.

In order to help with this understanding and transition, we have included a "computerized" section in this workbook. The computerized section is designed very simply; its purpose is to mirror what you learned and practiced in the manual section. You will see how the same transactions are handled with the computer software, and how much time is saved. But, by having completed the manual section first, you have the advantage of almost "seeing" what is going on "inside" the software. This gives you a great deal of understanding and ability especially when it comes to selecting software and designing back-up systems for the inevitable computer failures which you will encounter in your career.

③   **Please be sure to do the problems in the same order that they would be done during the hotel work day.** In the manual problems, don't try to do the transcript first, for example. Get the check-ins, the folios, and the voucher posting done first. If you do, you'll have a much better understanding of what's going on and the problems will be more fun and less time-consuming to do.

Manual Night Audit

Instructions and Exercises

Section 1

The Night Audit of Accounts Receivable

The purposes of performing the night audit include the following:

1.   ensure that each guest account is correct.

2.   ensure that charges and credits have been properly posted for accounting purposes, and

3.   provide succinct, valuable management reports summarizing the salient features of the day's business.

The methods used to fulfill these purposes are varied, but might be summarized into three major categories for simplicity's sake.

1.   **Manual methods**--the hand transcript. Very few of only the smallest lodging properties continue to use the hand transcript in practice. But, there are still some!

2.   **Electronic methods**--includes the use of posting machines (e.g., Micros, NCR, etc.) These systems generally require the maintenance of paper folios to be inserted into the posting machine each time a posting is to be done. Many of them, however, maintain each rooms's previous balance in memory, thus eliminating many of the so-called previous balance "pickup errors" which were so prevalent when the last generation of mechanical posting machines was phased out. The detail of each guest room account's accumulated transactions is maintained on the paper folio, just as in the manual system. The difference is that there's always a current balance on folio.

It should be noted, however, that there continue to be a few of the older mechanical systems around, such as the NCR 4200; use of such a system requires that particular attention be paid to auditing for previous balance pickup errors during the night audit, which could have been made on the day shifts.

3.   **Computer methods**--including both PC (personal computer) driven systems and main-frame systems.

   a.   PCs generally constitute small scale computer systems quite often integrating all front office functions including reservations and room status as well as the accounting functions for guests' accounts

2

receivable. Depending upon the size of the property and design of the system, the PC can operate as a stand alone computer or integrated on a Local Area Network (LAN).

b. Full scale, main-frame computer systems generally consist of a hotel wide system including many terminals and driven from one large central processing unit. The scope and use of these "main frame" systems is rapidly changing as the individual PCs and LANs become extremely powerful.

In the past, the PC and the main frame have been two very distinct types of computer systems. The last few years have seen tremendous advances in technology. These advances continue and in so doing allow small properties to begin with systems of the appropriate size and complexity for the property's small size. These systems also have the ability to expand both software and hardware to allow for growth in both business size and computer sophistication.

The concept of "networking" PCs together has virtually made the possibility of computer use desirable in almost any size or type property. Nevertheless, an understanding of the basic concepts as they are put forth in the manual system is crucial to making these evolving applications.

Finally, be prepared for many different applications in the field. While most hotel and lodging properties are at least partially computerized, there are still many, especially smaller ones, which are not. The principles of accuracy of guest bills, proper distribution of charges among operating departments, and availability of succinct management reports remain the same. Executing them becomes more efficient, faster, and simpler as computer applications become more sophisticated.

In any case, the following formula summarizes the requirements for the night audit to be satisfactorily completed regardless of which system is used.

THE NIGHT AUDIT FORMULA

THE CALCULATION	*THE PROOF*
TODAY'S OPENING GUEST LEDGER BALANCE (from folios)	(Must equal yesterday's closing balance.)
+ TODAY'S CHARGES (from folios)	(Must equal today's voucher totals for each department which must equal departmental control totals for each department.)
- TODAY'S CREDITS (from folios)	(Must equal today's voucher totals for each department, or cash, or transfers as appropriate and must equal any departmental control totals as appropriate.)
= TODAY'S CLOSING GUEST LEDGER BALANCE	(Must equal the total of the folio closing balances on folio balance sheet, tape or total.)

Immediately following the directions for student use, there is a sample job analysis for the manual night audit. It is included as a guideline in arriving at a management perspective concerning the night audit. It should serve as a reminder that similar outlines should be prepared for the night audit (or any front office job) regardless of what system is used to perform the audit. The analysis is a training aid and provides a measure of security for the new employee, especially the first few shifts she works by herself.

To be sure, the analysis included here is simply a sample. Most hotels have their own particular way of doing things. Yet, the basic procedures are undoubtedly common to all lodging facilities. Certainly, management could take the analysis further, fleshing it out to a full scale procedural manual by explaining each job analysis step in more detail and illustrating the steps with sample calculations, diagrams, forms and photographs.

In front office systems using electronic posting machines or computers, clearly labeled diagrams and photographs should illustrate the function and position of each key, switch or screen in the proper order. This is primarily for the benefit of the employee who is not familiar with the system, and so should be as simply and clearly stated as possible.

Most contemporary computer software should include optional "help" instructions directly in the program sequence thus making it as user-friendly as possible. By making the help screens optional, they are available when needed but not necessary to the function of the program, and thus do not slow down the seasoned user. More powerful graphics and expanded memory also make it possible for screen displays to be very illustrative and self-explanatory.

Finally, the analysis for the manual night audit should serve as an aid to the student who is going to complete one or more of the problem sets contained herein in conjunction with classroom lectures and any accompanying textbook and the completed sample night audit forms which follow the analysis.

Section 3

Directions for the Student Exercise

The *Front Office Operations and Night Audit Workbook* actually encapsulates the entire hotel day's work in the front office including check-ins, check-outs, postings and other transactions. You actually perform an entire day's front office transactions before beginning the audit itself. The preliminary front office guest management part of the exercise should put front office accounting operations into cycled perspective. For this reason, we strongly urge you to complete each problem in the order in which the components of that problem appear--as though you were working in the front office from the morning on through the day and evening shifts and finally ending with the night audit itself.

So, in order for you to realize the full benefit of the exercises it is best to approach it as realistically as possible. This means that the transactions should be made in roughly the same order in which they would chronologically happen. Thus all of the check-ins, check-outs, postings and other transactions should be completed prior to beginning the night audit procedure itself. You should refer to whichever main text or handouts you are using for the course as a guide for guest registration, folio preparation, etc.

In other words, you will, for the first part of the exercise, do the work of the day and swing shift receptionist and cashiers. You will then begin the work of the night auditor. At that point it would be beneficial to begin to use the sample "Job Analysis" as an instructional guide.

Section 4

Sample Job Analysis for the Manual Night Audit

1. Read log book and any new memos or communications.

2. Obtain any necessary information from the off-going shift.

3. Count cash (if using common bank with other shifts).

4. Post any charges which still remain from the previous shift.

5. Prepare the Room and House Count Report (if not done by a night clerk).

6. Total charge and credit vouchers by department and fasten an adding machine tape to each packet of vouchers.

7. Check voucher packet totals against departmental control sheet totals if available.

8.   a.   Post room and tax to each folio.
       b.   Add total charges, total credits and closing balance for each folio.
       c.   Post the charges and credits from each folio to the transcript sheet.

9. When all folios are posted to the transcript, add the total charges, the total credits, and the closing balance for each room entered on the transcript.

10. Foot and cross-foot the transcript (add rows across and columns down). This simply ensures that there are no mathematical errors; it does not mean the audit is in balance.

11. Verify that the departmental total columns on the transcript agree with the voucher totals (and with the departmental control sheet totals) for each department.

12. Make an adding machine tape which includes the closing balance of each guest ledger folio. The total of the tape is the guest ledger closing balance for the day.

13. Verify that the total guest ledger balance for today according to the adding machine tape of the folio closing balances agrees with the total, net guest ledger closing balance as shown on the transcript. The night audit is in balance if the totals indicated to this point agree.

14. Carry forward the closing balance for each room on today's transcript as the opening balance on tomorrow's transcript.

Section 5

Sample Night Audit Exercise for the University Inn

Introduction

*   This exercise is an example of performing the night audit.

*   Included at the end of the exercise are the completed cash sheet, cash envelope, room and house count sheet, and the transcript sheet.

*   Brief notes appear on these completed forms to help you understand how each document ties together. Of course you shouldn't write these notes on your forms when you do the subsequent problems.

****

Sample Exercise

Following are the guest ledger balances at the close of the night audit for April 24. They become the opening balances for April 25.

Room #	Guest Names	Opening Balance For April 25, 19__
202	Mr. Rocky Roach	$63.48
207	Mr. and Mrs. Phil Up	$12.25
208	Mr. Drew Down	$56.04
210	Mr. Stan Ipslinski	$74.00

The following are the summaries of the departmental control sheets and other transactions for April 25.

1.   Mr. Roach pays his account with cash and checks out. (After his charge is posted.)

2.   Mr. Down in 208 pays $70.00 on account and will stay another night. His room rents for $25.00.

3.   Mr. and Mrs. Francisco Ramos and child of No. 20 Forbes Park, Manila, Philippines check in to room 201 at $40.00 per night. They will stay 3 nights.

4.   Mr. Leonardo Da Vinci checks in to room 204. He had an advance deposit in the City Ledger of $38.50. He will stay 2 nights and is from 500 Broadway, New York, NY 10001. His rate is $35.00.

5.   Mr. and Mrs. Ramos have a tip paid-out to the restaurant for $1.50.

6.   Ms. Sadie Silver and Ms. Nelly Nod check in to room 206. The total room rate is $54.00. They are with the Kold Kreem Company of 1 Main Street, Union City, NJ 10033. They will stay one night.

7.   Rabbi Jacob Josephson checks in to room 209 for 1 week at the daily rate of $18.00. He is from 25 Park Place, New York, NY 10002.

8.   Mr. Ipslinski complains to the Assistant Manager that his shirt was not folded as he had requested, but was placed on a hanger instead. The Assistant Manager authorizes an allowance of $2.00 off his laundry charge from April 24.

9.   Mr. Ipslinski, in room 210, pays his account with an American Express credit card, and checks out. (There are no further charges.)

10. Mr. and Mrs. Conrad Vanderbuilt check in to room 210 for 1 week at the daily rate of $78.00 per day.   They have a $90.00 advance deposit in the City Ledger and reside at 201 Magnolia Lane, Oil City, TX 92543.

11. A C.O.D. package arrives for Mr. Vanderbuilt for which the cashier makes a $2.72 paid-out to the postman.

12. Mr. and Mrs. Up have requested that $6.40 of Mr. Down's bill be transferred to their account.

13. Mr. and Mrs. Up pay with traveler's checks after their charge is posted and check out.

14. Mr. and Mrs. Salvatore Fertilla and their 5 children check in to rooms 202/203. The total rate is $51.00. They will stay for one night and are from 27 Lombard Street, San Francisco, CA 88552.

15. Flowers from the Daisy Flower Shop arrive for Mr. Vanderbuilt for which the cashier makes a paid-out of $10.50.

16. Mr. and Mrs. Fertilla pay $125.00 on account.

17. Ms. Silver pays $6.27 on account.

18. Mr. and Mrs. Pat Moreo and child, of the University of Nevada, Las Vegas, check in to room 207. The room is an $18.00 special rate. They pay for 2 nights room and tax in advance with an approved personal check.

Restaurant Summary April 25, 199		Beverage Summary April 25, 199	
201 (Ramos)	$10.00	201 (Ramos)	$3.50
202 (Roach)	$3.75	204 (Da Vinci)	$7.80
202/3 (Fertilla)	$12.00	208 (Down)	$6.40
202/3 (Fertilla)	$38.00	206 (Nod)	$2.50
206 (Silver)	$6.19	210 (Vanderbuilt)	$42.85
210 (Vanderbuilt)	$120.00		
206 (Nod)	$7.01		
209 (Josephson)	$8.75		

Local Telephone Summary April 25,199		Long Distance Telephone Summary April 25,199	
204 (Da Vinci)	$0.20	202/3 (Fertilla)	$3.81
202/3 (Fertilla)	$0.60	206 (Silver)	$6.27
209 (Josephson)	$0.40	210 (Vanderbuilt)	$57.50
209 (Josephson)	$0.60	208 (Down)	$2.80
210 (Vanderbuilt)	$1.00	207 (Up)	$8.16
207 (Moreo)	$0.80	207 (Moreo)	$3.25

Notes:

1. Room tax is computed at 10%.

2. Room revenue for April 24 was $90.00.

3. Blank folios have been provided for the rooms which were occupied on April 24. You need not be concerned with addresses for these guests if none are given. Assume that they already have registration cards on file.

The following are the contents of the cash drawer at the close of business.

Personal Checks:		$125.00
		39.60
		67.23
Traveler Checks:		160.00
Bills:	$20.00	60.00
	$10.00	90.00
	$5.00	130.00
	$1.00	98.00
Coins:	.25	31.00
	.10	13.70
	.05	5.20
	.01	.46

The drawer started with a $500.00 bank.

Sample Night Audit Forms for the University Inn for this sample audit are shown on the following pages.

Sample Registration Cards

Folio #: _____

UNIVERSITY INN
Registration Card

Date April 25, 199_

Name **Francisco Ramos**
Street **No. 20 Forbes Park**
City **Manila**   State **Philippines**   Zip Code _____
Affiliation _____

Arrival Date	Room #	Rate	Clerk	Departure Date	Credit Card #
April 25, 199	201	$40	GS	April 28, 199_	

Remarks: 2 Adults, 1 child

Money, Jewels, and other Valuable Packages, must be placed in the Safe in the Office, otherwise the Management will not be responsible for any loss.

Cut along double lines   *Cut along double lines*

Folio #: _____

UNIVERSITY INN
Registration Card

Date April 25, 199_

Name **Leonardo Da Vinci**
Street **500 Broadway**
City **NYC**   State **NY**   Zip Code **10001**
Affiliation _____

Arrival Date	Room #	Rate	Clerk	Departure Date	Credit Card #
April 25, 199	204	$35	GS	April 27, 199_	

Remarks: Advance Deposit $38.50

Money, Jewels, and other Valuable Packages, must be placed in the Safe in the Office, otherwise the Management will not be responsible for any loss.

13

UNIVERSITY INN

Folio #: _____

Guest's Name: **Francisco Ramos** _____

Room #: **201** _____

Departure Date: **April 28, 199_** _____

Today's Date: **April 25, 199_** _____

ALL ACCOUNTS ARE DUE WHEN RENDERED

DATE	April 25	April 26					
FORWARD	$0.00	$59.00					
Room	40.00						
Tax	4.00						
Restaurant	10.00						
Beverages	3.50						
Telephone - Local							
Telephone - L.D.							
Laundry							
Valet							
Misc. Charges							
Cash Disbursements	1.50						
Transfer Debits							
TOTAL DEBITS	$59.00						
Cash Received							
Allowances							
Transfer to City Ledger							
Transfer Credit							
TOTAL CREDITS	$0.00						
BALANCE FORWARD	$59.00						

RESTAURANT DEPARTMENT CONTROL SHEET

NAME: Sample Audit   **DATE:** April 25, 199_

VOUCHER #	ROOM NO.	GUEST NAME	AMOUNT	MEMO
	201	Ramos	$10.00	
	202	Roach	$3.75	
	202/203	Fertilla	$12.00	
	202/203	Fertilla	$38.00	
	206	Silver	$6.19	
	210	Vanderbuilt	$120.00	
	206	Nod	$7.01	
	209	Josephson	$8.75	
Compares to Column #8 on				
Daily Transcript Sheet		Total Amount	$205.70	

BEVERAGE DEPARTMENT CONTROL SHEET

NAME: Sample Audit   **DATE:** April 25, 199_

VOUCHER #	ROOM NO.	GUEST NAME	AMOUNT	MEMO
	201	Ramos	$3.50	
	204	Da Vinci	$7.80	
	208	Down	$6.40	
	206	Nod	$2.50	
	210	Vanderbuilt	$42.85	
Compares to Column #8 on				
Daily Transcript Sheet		Total Amount	$63.05	

Sample Vouchers

No. 1001

Sample Audit

UNIVERSITY INN

Restaurant **Charge**

Department

Date: April 25, 199_

Name Rabbi Jacob Josephso   Room or Acct. No. **209**

Date	Symbol	Amount
Do not write in above space		
		$8.75

EXPLANATION
Dinner

Signed by: *GS*

Cut along double lines.

No. 1002

Sample Audit

UNIVERSITY INN

Cash Disbursement (Tip) **Charge**

Department

Date: April 25, 199_

Name Francisco Ramos   Room or Acct. No. **201**

Date	Symbol	Amount
Do not write in above space		
		$1.50

EXPLANATION
Paid out tip to K.T. in restaurant

Signed by: *GS*

Cut along double lines.

No. 1003

Sample Audit

UNIVERSITY INN

Transfer **Credit**

Department

Date: April 25, 199_

Name Mr. & Mrs. Phil Up   Room or Acct. No. **208**

Date	Symbol	Amount
Do not write in above space		
		($6.40)

EXPLANATION
Transfer $6.40 from Mr. Down's (Room 208)

Signed by: *GS*

No. 1004

Sample Audit

UNIVERSITY INN

Transfer **Credit**

Department

Date: April 25, 199_

Name Leonardo Da Vinci   Room or Acct. No. **204**

Date	Symbol	Amount
Do not write in above space		
		($38.50)

EXPLANATION
Transfer advance deposit from city ledger.

Signed by: *GS*

19

UNIVERSITY INN
FRONT OFFICE CASH SHEET
Sample Audit

Date: April 25, 199___

Cash Receipts			Cash Disbursements - Guests			
Room	Name	Amount	Room	Name	Item	Amount
202	Mr. Rocky Roach	$67.23	201	M/M Ramos	Tip/Rest	$1.50
208	Mr. Drew Down	$70.00	210	Mr. C. Vanderbuilt	C.O.D.	$2.72
207	M/M Phil Up	$26.81	210	Mr. C. Vanderbuilt	Flowers	$10.50
202/3	M/M S. Fertila	$125.00				
206	Ms. S. Silver	$6.27				
207	M/M P. Moreo	$39.60				
				Guest Disbursements Subtotal		$14.72

Cash Disbursements - House

	House Disbursements Subtotal	$0.00

RECAPITULATION

	Total Cash Receipts	$334.91
	Disbursements - Guests	$14.72
+	Disbursements - House	$0.00
-	Total Disbursements	$14.72

Cash Receipts Total	$334.91	= **Deposit**	$320.19

Agrees with Cash Disbursement on Transcript

Agrees with Column 17
Cash Receipts on the Daily Transcript

Agrees with Deposit on Cash Turn-In Envelope

Sample Cash Turn-in Envelope and Closing Bank Count

UNIVERSITY INN
CLOSING BANK COUNT
Sample Audit

Cashier Name:	Gail Sammons
Cashier Shift:	Swing
Date:	April 25, 199

Bills:	$100.00	
	50.00	
	20.00	60.00
	10.00	90.00
	5.00	130.00
	1.00	98.00
Coins:	.50	
	.25	31.00
	.10	13.70
	.05	5.20
	.01	0.46
	Sub Total	$428.36
+	Due Back	$71.64
=	TOTAL BANK	$500.00

Due back on Cash Turn-In Envelope

Agrees with Due back on Closing Bank Count Sheet

Agrees with Deposit on Front Office Cash Sheet

This envelope is deposited in safe at the end of shift.

UNIVERSITY INN
CASH TURN-IN ENVELOPE
Sample Audit

Cashier Name:	Gail Sammons
Cashier Shift:	Swing
Date:	April 25, 199

Bills:	$100.00	
	50.00	
	20.00	
	10.00	
	5.00	
	1.00	
Coins:	.50	
	.25	
	.10	
	.05	
	.01	

Checks and Vouchers

Personal Check	125.00
Personal Check	39.60
Personal Check	67.23
Travelers Checks	160.00
Total Amount Enclosed	$391.83
- DUE BACK	$71.64
= DEPOSIT	$320.19
- DEPOSIT (from cash sheet)	$320.19
DIFFERENCE (over/short)	$0.00

23

Sample Room and House Count Sheet

UNIVERSITY INN
ROOM AND HOUSE COUNT SHEET
Sample Audit

Date: April 25, 199___

Room Reconciliation

	No. of Rooms	No. of Persons	Room Value	Tax Value
Yesterday	4	5	$90.00	$9.00
+ Arrivals	8	19	294	29.4
= Total	12	24	384	38.4
- Departures	3	4	65	6.5
= Today	9	20	$319.00	$31.90

Agrees with Totals for columns 3, 5, and 6 respectively on transcript.

Room Statistics

Rooms Available	10
Rooms Occupied	9
House Count	20
Average Rate per Occupied Room	$35.44
Average Rate per Guest	$15.95
Percentage of Occupancy	90.0%
Average Number of Guests per Room	2.2

Usually prepared from room rack.

Room #	No. of Guests	Tax	Room Rate
201	3	$4.00	$40.00
202/3	7	5.10	51.00
203	See Room 202		
204	1	3.50	35.00
205			
206	2	5.40	54.00
207	3	1.80	18.00
208	1	2.50	25.00
209	1	1.80	18.00
210	2	7.80	78.00
TOTAL	$20.00	$31.90	$319.00

Agrees with Totals for columns 3, 5, and 6 respectively on transcript.

Sample Daily Transcript
University Inn

Daily Transcript of Guest Ledger (Sample Audit)

1	2	3	4	5	6	7	8	9	10	11	12	13	14	15	16	17	18	19	20	21	22
Folio No.	Room No.	No. of Guests	Opening Balance DB (CR)	Room	Room Tax	Restaurant	Beverages	Local Calls	Long Distance	Laundry	Valet	Misc. Charge	Cash Disburse.	Transfer Debit	Total Daily Charges	Cash Receipts	Allowances	Transfer to City Ledger	Transfer Credit	Total Credits	Closing Balance
	201	3		40.00	4.00	10.00	3.50						1.50		59.00	0.00				0.00	59.00
	202	7		51.00	5.10	50.00		0.60	3.81						110.51	125.00				125.00	-14.49
	203	See 202																			0.00
	204	1		35.00	3.50		7.80	0.20							46.50				38.50	38.50	8.00
	205																				0.00
	206	2		54.00	5.40	13.20	2.50		6.27						81.37	6.27				6.27	75.10
	207	3		18.00	1.80			0.80	3.25						23.85	39.60				39.60	-15.75
	208	1	56.04	25.00	2.50		6.40		2.80						36.70	70.00			6.40	76.40	16.34
	209	1		18.00	1.80	8.75		1.00							29.55					0.00	29.55
	210	2		78.00	7.80	120.00	42.85	1.00	57.50				13.22		320.37				90.00	90.00	230.37
Sub Total		20	56.04	319.00	31.90	201.95	63.05	3.60	73.63	0.00	0.00	0.00	14.72	0.00	707.85	240.87	0.00	0.00	134.90	375.77	**388.12**
DEPARTURES																					
	202		63.48			3.75									3.75	67.23				67.23	-0.00
	207		12.25						8.16					6.4	14.56	26.81				26.81	0.00
	210		74														2.00	72.00		74.00	0.00
Sub Total			149.73			3.75			8.16					6.4	18.31	94.04	2.00	72.00	0.00	168.04	-0.00
GRAND TOTAL HOUSE			205.77	319.00	31.90	205.70	63.05	3.60	81.79	0.00	0.00	0.00	14.72	6.4	726.16	334.91	2.00	72.00	134.90	543.81	**388.12**

Agrees with Total of all Current Folios added together

Agrees with Voucher Totals for each Column

Agrees with Total Receipts from Cash Sheet

Agrees with Guest Cash Disbursement from Cash Sheet

Agrees with Voucher Totals

Agrees with Voucher Totals for Each Department AND with Departmental Control Sheets for Each Department

Agrees with Room & House Count Sheet

Agrees with Yesterday's Daily Balance

Section 6

Night Audit Exercise for the University Inn

Problem Set No. I

Introduction

*   This exercise consists of performing the night audit using the hand transcript for the 10 room University Inn for the 13th of November, 199_.

*   Please read this <u>entire</u> sheet <u>before</u> you begin the exercise.

****

Exercise

Following are the guest ledger balances at the close of the night audit for November 12.   They become the opening balances for November 13.

Room #	Guest Names	Opening Balance For November 13, 199_
202	Mr. Rocky Roach	$47.18
207	Mr. and Mrs. Phil Up	$12.25
208	Mr. Drew Down	$56.04
210	Mr. Stan Ipslinski	$64.00

Following are summaries of the departmental control sheets and other transactions for November 13:

1.   Mr. Roach pays his account in cash and checks out. (After his charge is posted.)

2.   Mr. Down in 208 pays $70.00 on account and will stay another night. His room rents for $30.00.

3.   Mr. and Mrs. Francisco Ramos and child of No. 20 Forbes Park, Manila, Philippines check in to room 201 at $40.00 per night. They will stay 3 nights.

4. Mr. Leonardo Da Vinci checks in to room 204. He had an advance deposit in the City Ledger of $27.50. He will stay 2 nights and is from 500 Broadway, New York, NY 10001. His rate is $25.00.

5. Ms. Sadie Silver and Ms. Nelly Nod check in to room 206. The total room rate is $46.00. They are with the Kold Kreem Company of 1 Main Street, Union City, NJ 10011. They will stay one night.

6. Mr. and Mrs. Ramos have a tip paid-out to the restaurant for $1.50.

7. Rabbi Jacob Josephson checks in to room 209 for 1 week at the daily rate of $18.00. He is from 25 Park Place, New York, NY 10002.

8. Mr. Ipslinski complains to the Assistant Manager that his shirt was not folded as he had requested, but was placed on a hangar instead. The Assistant Manager authorizes an allowance of $2.00 off his laundry charge from November 12.

9. Mr. Ipslinski, in room 210, pays his account with an American Express credit card, and checks out.

10. Mr. and Mrs. Conrad Vanderbuilt check in to room 210 for 1 week at the daily rate of $78.00 per day. They have an $86.00 advance deposit in the City Ledger and reside at 201 Magnolia Lane, Oil City, TX 92543.

11. A C.O.D. package arrives for Mr. Vanderbuilt for which the cashier makes a $6.72 paid-out to the postman.

12. Mr. and Mrs. Up have requested that $6.40 of Mr. Down's bill be transferred to their account.

13. Mr. and Mrs. Up pay with traveler's checks after their charge is posted and check out.

14. Mr. and Mrs. Salvatore Fertilla and their 5 children check in to rooms 202/203. The total rate is $48.00. They will stay for one night and are from 27 Lombard Street, San Francisco, CA 88552.

15. Flowers from the Daisy Flower Shop arrive for Mr. Vanderbuilt for which the cashier makes a paid-out of $10.50.

16. Mr. and Mrs. Fertilla pay $125.00 on account.

17. Ms. Silver pays $6.27 on account.

29

18. Mr. and Mrs. Pat Moreo and child, of the University of Nevada, Las Vegas, check in to room 207. The room is an $18.00 special rate. They pay for 2 nights room and tax in advance with an approved personal check.

Restaurant Summary November 13, 199			Beverage Summary November 13, 199		
201	(Ramos)	$10.00	201	(Ramos)	$3.50
202	(Roach)	$3.75	204	(Da Vinci)	$7.80
202/3	(Fertilla)	$12.00	208	(Down)	$6.40
202/3	(Fertilla)	$38.00	206	(Nod)	$2.50
206	(Silver)	$5.95	210	(Vanderbuilt)	$34.15
206	(Nod)	$7.01			
210	(Vanderbuilt)	$120.00			
209	(Josephson)	$8.75			

Local Telephone Summary November 13, 199			Long Distance Telephone Summary November 13, 199		
204	(Da Vinci)	$0.20	202/3	(Fertilla)	$3.81
202/3	(Fertilla)	$0.60	206	(Silver)	$6.27
209	(Josephson)	$0.40	210	(Vanderbuilt)	$57.50
209	(Josephson)	$0.60	208	(Down)	$2.80
210	(Vanderbuilt)	$1.00	207	(Up)	$8.16
207	(Moreo)	$0.80	207	(Moreo)	$3.25

Notes:

1. Room tax is computed at 10%.

2. Room revenue for November 12 was 90.00.

3. Blank folios have been provided for the rooms which were occupied on November 12. You need not be concerned with addresses for these guests if none are given. Assume that they already have registration cards on file.

The following are the contents of the cash drawer at the close of business.

Personal Checks: $125.00
                                            39.60
                                            50.93
Traveler Checks: 160.00
Bills: $20.00   60.00
                $10.00   90.00
                 $5.00   130.00
                 $1.00   94.00
Coins: .25   31.00
                  .10   13.70
                  .05   5.20
                  .01   .46

The drawer started with a $500.00 bank.

Section 7

Night Audit Exercise for the University Inn

Problem Set No. II

Introduction

* This exercise consists of performing the night audit using the hand transcript for the 10 room University Inn for the 14th of November 199_.

* This problem set is designed to be used by students as a stand alone exercise or as a follow up exercise to Problem I. The opening balances are as follows for November 14.

****

Exercise

Room #	Guest Names	Opening Balance For November 14, 199_
201	Mr. and Mrs. F. Ramos	$59.00
202/203	Mr. and Mrs. S. Fertilla	($17.79)
204	Mr. and Mrs. L. Da Vinci	$8.00
206	Ms. S. Silver	$31.25
206	Ms. N. Nod	$34.81
207	Mr. and Mrs. P. Moreo	($15.75)
208	Mr. D. Down	$21.84
209	Rabbi J. Josephson	$29.55
210	Mr. and Mrs. C. Vanderbuilt	$229.67

Following are the transactions and summaries of the departmental charges for November 14.

1. Dr. and Mrs. John Rhodes check in to Room 205. Their address is UC Davis, CA 89623. The room rate is $117 per night. They had an advance deposit of $128.70. In addition, they pay another $250 in traveler's checks on account.

2.   Mr. Down checks out of room 208. He pays his account with traveler's checks.

3.   The Fertilla family checks out of 202/203 with no further charges. Their credit balance must be returned to them.

4.   Mr. and Mrs. Moreo check out of room 207 (one night early). They ask that $8.75 which was charged to Josephson's account in room 209 be transferred to their account first. They have a tip paid-out for $3. They pay their balance in cash.

5.   Ms. Elaine Martucci of the Marine Midland Trust Co., Rochester, NY 14000 checks in to room 203. The rate is $84 per night. She will pay with Visa.

6.   Ms. Nod and Ms. Silver check out of room 206. Nod pays her account with cash. Silver pays with Visa.

7.   Dr. Rhodes has a miscellaneous paid-out of $7.25 for a FAX sent to U.C. Davis.

8.   Mr. Ramos in Room 201 has a C.O.D. delivery of theater tickets arrive for which he has authorized a paid-out amount of $96.

9.   Mr. Da Vinci checks out of room 204. He pays his account with a Diner's Club card.

10.   Mr. Richard Sullivan of 1701 Mission Vista Drive, San Diego, CA 87524, checks in to room 204. The rate is $60 per night. He will pay with an American Express.

11.   Mr. Sullivan of room 204 has a tip paid-out of $2.50.

12.   Mr. Vanderbuilt of room 210 has a tip paid-out for $4.

13.   Dr. Marie and Mr. Anthony Lucca of Temple University, Philadelphia, PA 12201, check in to room 208 at a nightly rate of $110. They had an advance reservation deposit of $121. They will pay the remainder of their account with Master Card.

14.   Ms. Stephanie Baumweiss checks in to room 202. Her address is Van Camps Publishing Co., McCormick Place, Chicago, IL 66220. She will stay one night at a $68 room rate. She will be a direct billing.

15.   Mr. Oscar Lopez and Mr. George Whipple of the Washington Publishing Co., 718 Broadway, New York, NY 10001, check in to room 207. They are unsure of how many nights they will stay. Mr. Lopez will pay with an American Express Card, and Mr. Whipple will pay with a Master Card. The room rate is $80 per night.

16.   Mr. Lucca of room 208 has a $7 tip paid-out.

17. Mr. Harvey Shade of 807 Main Street, Frisbee, OH 32221, checks in to room 206 at a rate of $62 per night. He will stay 2 nights; he will pay in cash. He anticipates charges and so pays $200 on account.

18. Mr. Vanderbuilt asked to look at his account and tells us that he did not get through on one of the long distance calls for which he was billed yesterday. The assistant front office manager authorizes a Long Distance Telephone Adjustment of $4.80.

Restaurant Summary November 14, 199			Beverage Summary November 14, 199		
207	(Moreo)	$15.85	210	(Vanderbuilt)	$32.00
206	(Silver)	$4.50	201	(Ramos)	$4.20
201	(Ramos)	$18.95	207	(Lopez)	$7.00
204	(Da Vinci)	$6.50	203	(Martucci)	$27.86
204	(Sullivan)	$15.50	207	(Whipple)	$6.85
208	(Lucca)	$40.00			
210	(Vanderbuilt)	$478.00			
205	(Rhodes)	$68.00			

Local Telephone Summary November 14, 199			Long Distance Telephone Summary November 14, 199		
204	(Da Vinci)	$2.00	206	(Nod)	$6.78
204	(Sullivan)	$0.80	204	(Da Vinci)	$10.60
210	(Vanderbuilt)	$3.40	201	(Ramos)	$1.80
203	(Martucci)	$1.60	203	(Martucci)	$4.55
208	(Lucca)	$1.00			

Notes:
1. Room tax is computed at 10%.

2. Room revenue for November 13 was $303.

3. If you have not done Problem Set I, you will need to prepare folios for those guests already registered from November 13.

The following are the contents of the cash drawer at the close of business.

Personal Checks:		$250.00; 200.00
Traveler Checks:		220.00
Bills:	$20.00	40.00
	$10.00	80.00
	$5.00	30.00
	$1.00	42.00
Coins:	.25	12.25
	.10	5.20
	.05	3.55
	.01	.96

The drawer started with a $500.00 bank.

Section 8

Night Audit Exercise for the University Inn

Problem Set No. III

Introduction

* This exercise consists of performing the night audit using the hand transcript for the 10 room University Inn for the 27th of May 199_.

* This problem set is designed to be used by students as a stand alone exercise. Following are guest ledger balances at the close of the night audit for May 26, 199_. They become the opening balances for May 27.

****

Exercise

Room #	Guest Names	Opening Balance For May 27, 199_
201	Bliss, V. / Chapman, P.	$250.00
202	Hope, G.	$80.00
203	Jones, T.	$65.00
204	Cook, S.	$42.00
205	Spencer, C.	$64.50
205	Jensen, J.	$69.50
206	Halvorson, P.	$92.00

The following are transactions for the University Inn on May 27, 199_.

1. Mrs. Bliss & Mrs. Chapman decide to leave three days early. They were to stay two weeks, but the weather has been cold and rainy so they have decided to check out early. They want to split the bill in half. Mrs. Bliss will pay by cash and Mrs. Chapman will pay by VISA. (After their charges are posted.)

36

2. J. Sherwood from 202 Cherry Lane, Saginaw MI 55533 checks in to room 201. She requests secure parking for her car and is willing to pay the $25.00 parking fee. She requests a safety deposit box and the clerk informs her about the in-room safe. Mrs. Sherwood will stay for three nights. The room rate will be $50.00 per night.

3. Ms. G. Hope pays her account in cash and check-out. (After her charge is posted.)

4. Mr. Spencer and Mr. Jensen come to the front desk to check out. After their charges are posted, Jensen notices a bar charge for $5.00 that was posted in error to his account instead of Spencer's account. The front desk clerk corrects the error. Spencer pays his account by personal check and Jensen pays by Master Card.

5. Ms. Sherwood pays $100 in cash on her account.

6. Mr. P. Halvorson complains about his laundry charge of $10.00 for four shirts. One shirt was not pressed properly and the other one was folded instead of placed on a hangar. The front desk manager authorizes an allowance of $5.00.

7. Mr. & Mrs. Tom Pledger and granddaughter check into room 207. Their address is 4500 Harvest Time, Odessa, TX 99345. They request a roll-away for their granddaughter. They will be staying for two nights. The room rate for room 207 is $45.00 plus the roll-away charge. Mr. Pledger will pay his account by American Express.

8. Mr. Halvorson in room 206 checks out. He pays his balance in cash.

9. Mr. T. Jones checks out. He wants to direct bill his company for room and restaurant charges. The address is IBM Corp. 221 IBM Drive, Computer City, MN 54545. He will pay the telephone charges posted to his bill in cash.

10. Mr. & Mrs. Yamonoto and 4 children check into adjoining rooms 209 and 210 for one week. Two of the children are 14 or older. The room charge is $40.00 per room. They have an advance deposit of $100.00.

11. A C.O.D. package arrives for J. Sherwood. The cashier pays out $7.50 to the postal delivery person.

12. Mr. & Mrs. Stephanopolous and baby check in for a two night stay. They would like the King Suite (room 207) at the government rate of $48.00. Their address is 202 Administrative Court, Washington, DC 44342. They request a crib.

13. Mr. Yamanoto pays $150.00 on account in traveler's checks.

14.   Flowers from the University Florist arrive for Mrs. Stephanopolous from her husband. The cashier pays out $22.50 for the flowers. ᵔ

15   Mr. S. Cook, room 204, request a late check-out. The front desk clerk explains the policy to charge $20.00 late check-out fee so Mr. Cook decides to leave at check-out time. He pays by Diner's Club after his charges are posted.

16.   Dan Lindseth from 203 Mountain View, Bynum, MT 59922 checks into room 208 at 3:00 pm. He is with Gateway Computers. His room rate is the corporate rate of $39.00.

17.   The Minute Only Laundry delivers laundry for Mr. Yamanoto. The charge is $15.00. The cashier does not have to pay out the $15.00 due to the direct bill agreement between the hotel and the laundry. The laundry charge is posted to Mr. Yamanoto's room.

18.   A fax is received at 4:00 pm for Mr. Lindseth. A miscellaneous charge of $3.00 for the fax is posted to his account. The clerk contacts Mr. Lindseth and he comes down to the desk to get his fax.

19.   At 5:00 pm, Mr. Lindseth comes down to check out. He has received an urgent message to return home at once. He signs his bill, explaining he has had three long distance phone calls, two local phone calls, and a restaurant charge. He leaves immediately.

20.   River High Wrestling team from River High School, Riverville, PA 16666, checks in at 5:00 pm for three nights. They have four rooms reserved: 202, 203, 204, and 205. The two coaches will stay in rooms 202 and 204 and the eight wrestlers will stay in rooms 203 and 205. No outgoing phone calls are to be allowed from rooms 203 and 205. All incoming calls should be forwarded to Mr. Volk in room 202. Mr. Wagon will be in room 204. The coaches' rooms will be $25.00 per night and the wrestling teams' rooms will be $40.00 per night.

21.   At 6:00 pm phone calls were received from room 203 and 205 requesting outside lines for local phone calls. The callers are told to contact their coach in room 202 to make those calls.

22.   Mr. Volk from room 202 would like to have a team meal at 10:00 pm. He would like to stay within his budget and pay only $4.50 per person. The front desk arranges the meal with the restaurant and makes out the charge and posts it. All restaurant charges for River High Wrestling team are to be posted to room 202.

23.   Mr. Volk, room 202 pays $200.00 on account with a School District #9 check.

24.   The cashier pays out a restaurant tip to Sue Worker for $7.50. The tip was from Yamanoto's restaurant bill and is posted to his room.

Restaurant Summary May 27, 199___		
201	Bliss/Chapman	$7.00
201	Sherwood	$5.50
205	Jensen	$10.00
205	Spencer	$7.50
201	Sherwood	$15.00
203	Jones	$5.00
204	Cook	$3.00
204	Cook	$4.00
208	Lindseth	$7.50
209	Yamanoto	$55.00

Beverage Summary May 27, 199___		
201	Sherwood	$5.50
205	Spencer	$15.00
209	Yamanoto	$20.00
201	Sherwood	$6.00
207	Stephanopolous	$25.00

Local Telephone Summary May 27, 199___		
201	Bliss/Chapman	$1.00
202	Hope	$0.50
205	Spencer	$0.50
201	Sherwood	$0.50
205	Jensen	$1.50
203	Jones	$0.50
208	Lindseth	$0.50
208	Lindseth	$0.50
202	Volk	$0.50
202	Volk	$0.50
202	Volk	$0.50
202	Volk	$0.50

Long Distance Telephone Summary May 27, 199___		
201	Bliss/Chapman	$4.00
202	Hope	$3.50
205	Jensen	$2.25
201	Sherwood	$7.50
203	Jones	$4.50
204	Cook	$5.00
208	Lindseth	$3.00
208	Lindseth	$4.50
202	Volk	$2.50
202	Volk	$5.50
209	Yamanoto	$5.00

Notes:

1.　Roll-away charge is $15.00 per night.

2.　Crib Charge is $5.00 per night.

3.　Room tax is 15%.

4.　Room revenue for March 29 was $120.00.

5.　Room 201 - Room rate for tonight is $50.00.

6.　Blank folios have been provided for the rooms which were occupied on May 26. You need not be concerned with addresses for these guests if none are given. Assume they already have registration cards on file.

The following are the contents of the cash drawer at the close of business.

Personal Checks:		Spencer School District #9
Traveler's Checks:		$200.00
Bills:	$100.00	$400.00
	20.00	220.00
	10.00	110.00
	5.00	55.00
	1.00	24.00
Coins:	$.25	$3.50
	.10	2.80
	.05	.95
	.01	.35

The drawer started with a $500.00 bank.

UNIVERSITY INN
Registration Card

Folio #:_____

Date_____

Name_____
Street_____
City_____ State_____ Zip Code_____
Affiliation_____

Arrival Date	Room #	Rate	Clerk	Departure Date	Credit Card #

Remarks: _____
_____
_____

Money, Jewels, and other Valuable Packages, must be placed in the Safe in the Office, otherwise the Management will not be responsible for any loss.

Cut along double lines   *Cut along double lines*

UNIVERSITY INN
Registration Card

Folio #:_____

Date_____

Name_____
Street_____
City_____ State_____ Zip Code_____
Affiliation_____

Arrival Date	Room #	Rate	Clerk	Departure Date	Credit Card #

Remarks: _____
_____
_____

Money, Jewels, and other Valuable Packages, must be placed in the Safe in the Office, otherwise the Management will not be responsible for any loss.

UNIVERSITY INN
Registration Card

Folio #:_____

Date_____

Name_____

Street_____

City_____ State_____ Zip Code_____

Affiliation_____

Arrival Date	Room #	Rate	Clerk	Departure Date	Credit Card #

Remarks: _____

_____

_____

Money, Jewels, and other Valuable Packages, must be placed in the Safe in the Office, otherwise the Management will not be responsible for any loss.

Cut along double lines   Cut along double lines

UNIVERSITY INN
Registration Card

Folio #:_____

Date_____

Name_____

Street_____

City_____ State_____ Zip Code_____

Affiliation_____

Arrival Date	Room #	Rate	Clerk	Departure Date	Credit Card #

Remarks: _____

_____

_____

Money, Jewels, and other Valuable Packages, must be placed in the Safe in the Office, otherwise the Management will not be responsible for any loss.

UNIVERSITY INN
Registration Card

Folio #:_____

Date_____

Name_____
Street_____
City_____ State_____ Zip Code_____
Affiliation_____

Arrival Date	Room #	Rate	Clerk	Departure Date	Credit Card #

Remarks: _____
_____
_____

Money, Jewels, and other Valuable Packages, must be placed in the Safe in the Office, otherwise the Management will not be responsible for any loss.

Cut along double lines   *Cut along double lines*

Folio #:_____

UNIVERSITY INN
Registration Card

Date_____

Name_____
Street_____
City_____ State_____ Zip Code_____
Affiliation_____

Arrival Date	Room #	Rate	Clerk	Departure Date	Credit Card #

Remarks: _____
_____
_____

Money, Jewels, and other Valuable Packages, must be placed in the Safe in the Office, otherwise the Management will not be responsible for any loss.

Folio #: _____

UNIVERSITY INN
Registration Card

Date _____

Name _____
Street _____
City _____ State _____ Zip Code _____
Affiliation _____

Arrival Date	Room #	Rate	Clerk	Departure Date	Credit Card #

Remarks: _____
_____
_____

Money, Jewels, and other Valuable Packages, must be placed in the Safe in the Office, otherwise the Management will not be responsible for any loss.

Cut along double lines   *Cut along double lines*

Folio #: _____

UNIVERSITY INN
Registration Card

Date _____

Name _____
Street _____
City _____ State _____ Zip Code _____
Affiliation _____

Arrival Date	Room #	Rate	Clerk	Departure Date	Credit Card #

Remarks: _____
_____
_____

Money, Jewels, and other Valuable Packages, must be placed in the Safe in the Office, otherwise the Management will not be responsible for any loss.

UNIVERSITY INN
Registration Card

Folio #:_____

Date_____

Name_____
Street_____
City_____ State_____ Zip Code_____
Affiliation_____

Arrival Date	Room #	Rate	Clerk	Departure Date	Credit Card #

Remarks: _____
_____
_____

Money, Jewels, and other Valuable Packages, must be placed in the Safe in the Office, otherwise the Management will not be responsible for any loss.

Cut along double lines   Cut along double lines

UNIVERSITY INN
Registration Card

Folio #:_____

Date_____

Name_____
Street_____
City_____ State_____ Zip Code_____
Affiliation_____

Arrival Date	Room #	Rate	Clerk	Departure Date	Credit Card #

Remarks: _____
_____
_____

Money, Jewels, and other Valuable Packages, must be placed in the Safe in the Office, otherwise the Management will not be responsible for any loss.

UNIVERSITY INN
Registration Card

Folio #:_____

Date_____

Name_____

Street_____

City_____ State_____ Zip Code_____

Affiliation_____

Arrival Date	Room #	Rate	Clerk	Departure Date	Credit Card #

Remarks: _____

_____

_____

Money, Jewels, and other Valuable Packages, must be placed in the Safe in the Office, otherwise the Management will not be responsible for any loss.

Cut along double lines   Cut along double lines

UNIVERSITY INN
Registration Card

Folio #:_____

Date_____

Name_____

Street_____

City_____ State_____ Zip Code_____

Affiliation_____

Arrival Date	Room #	Rate	Clerk	Departure Date	Credit Card #

Remarks: _____

_____

_____

Money, Jewels, and other Valuable Packages, must be placed in the Safe in the Office, otherwise the Management will not be responsible for any loss.

UNIVERSITY INN
Registration Card

Folio #: _____

Date _____

Name _____
Street _____
City _____ State _____ Zip Code _____
Affiliation _____

Arrival Date	Room #	Rate	Clerk	Departure Date	Credit Card #

Remarks: _____
_____
_____

Money, Jewels, and other Valuable Packages, must be placed in the Safe in the Office, otherwise the Management will not be responsible for any loss.

Cut along double lines   *Cut along double lines*

UNIVERSITY INN
Registration Card

Folio #: _____

Date _____

Name _____
Street _____
City _____ State _____ Zip Code _____
Affiliation _____

Arrival Date	Room #	Rate	Clerk	Departure Date	Credit Card #

Remarks: _____
_____
_____

Money, Jewels, and other Valuable Packages, must be placed in the Safe in the Office, otherwise the Management will not be responsible for any loss.

Folio #: _____

UNIVERSITY INN
Registration Card

Date _____

Name _____
Street _____
City _____ State _____ Zip Code _____
Affiliation _____

Arrival Date	Room #	Rate	Clerk	Departure Date	Credit Card #

Remarks: _____
_____
_____

Money, Jewels, and other Valuable Packages, must be placed in the Safe in the Office, otherwise the Management will not be responsible for any loss.

Cut along double lines   *Cut along double lines*

Folio #: _____

UNIVERSITY INN
Registration Card

Date _____

Name _____
Street _____
City _____ State _____ Zip Code _____
Affiliation _____

Arrival Date	Room #	Rate	Clerk	Departure Date	Credit Card #

Remarks: _____
_____
_____

Money, Jewels, and other Valuable Packages, must be placed in the Safe in the Office, otherwise the Management will not be responsible for any loss.

UNIVERSITY INN
Registration Card

Folio #:_____

Date_____

Name_____
Street_____
City_____ State_____ Zip Code_____
Affiliation_____

Arrival Date	Room #	Rate	Clerk	Departure Date	Credit Card #

Remarks: _____
_____
_____

Money, Jewels, and other Valuable Packages, must be placed in the Safe in the Office, otherwise the Management will not be responsible for any loss.

Cut along double lines   *Cut along double lines*

UNIVERSITY INN
Registration Card

Folio #:_____

Date_____

Name_____
Street_____
City_____ State_____ Zip Code_____
Affiliation_____

Arrival Date	Room #	Rate	Clerk	Departure Date	Credit Card #

Remarks: _____
_____
_____

Money, Jewels, and other Valuable Packages, must be placed in the Safe in the Office, otherwise the Management will not be responsible for any loss.

UNIVERSITY INN
Registration Card

Folio #: _____

Date _____

Name _____

Street _____

City _____ State _____ Zip Code _____

Affiliation _____

Arrival Date	Room #	Rate	Clerk	Departure Date	Credit Card #

Remarks: _____
_____
_____
_____

Money, Jewels, and other Valuable Packages, must be placed in the Safe in the Office, otherwise the Management will not be responsible for any loss.

Cut along double lines   *Cut along double lines*

UNIVERSITY INN
Registration Card

Folio #: _____

Date _____

Name _____

Street _____

City _____ State _____ Zip Code _____

Affiliation _____

Arrival Date	Room #	Rate	Clerk	Departure Date	Credit Card #

Remarks: _____
_____
_____
_____

Money, Jewels, and other Valuable Packages, must be placed in the Safe in the Office, otherwise the Management will not be responsible for any loss.

UNIVERSITY INN

Folio #: _____

Guest's Name: _____   Room #: _____

Departure Date: _____   Today's Date: _____

ALL ACCOUNTS ARE DUE WHEN RENDERED

DATE							
FORWARD							
Room							
Tax							
Restaurant							
Beverages							
Telephone - Local							
Telephone - L.D.							
Laundry							
Valet							
Misc. Charges							
Cash Disbursements							
Transfer Debits							
TOTAL DEBITS							
Cash Received							
Allowances							
Transfer to City Ledger							
Transfer Credit							
TOTAL CREDITS							
BALANCE FORWARD							

UNIVERSITY INN

Folio #: _____

Guest's Name: _____   Room #: _____

Departure Date: _____   Today's Date: _____

ALL ACCOUNTS ARE DUE WHEN RENDERED

DATE							
FORWARD							
Room							
Tax							
Restaurant							
Beverages							
Telephone - Local							
Telephone - L.D.							
Laundry							
Valet							
Misc. Charges							
Cash Disbursements							
Transfer Debits							
TOTAL DEBITS							
Cash Received							
Allowances							
Transfer to City Ledger							
Transfer Credit							
TOTAL CREDITS							
BALANCE FORWARD							

UNIVERSITY INN

Folio #: _____

Guest's Name: _____   Room #: _____

Departure Date: _____   Today's Date: _____

ALL ACCOUNTS ARE DUE WHEN RENDERED

DATE							
FORWARD							
Room							
Tax							
Restaurant							
Beverages							
Telephone - Local							
Telephone - L.D.							
Laundry							
Valet							
Misc. Charges							
Cash Disbursements							
Transfer Debits							
TOTAL DEBITS							
Cash Received							
Allowances							
Transfer to City Ledger							
Transfer Credit							
TOTAL CREDITS							
BALANCE FORWARD							

UNIVERSITY INN

Folio #: _____

Guest's Name: _____   Room #: _____

Departure Date: _____   Today's Date: _____

ALL ACCOUNTS ARE DUE WHEN RENDERED

DATE							
FORWARD							
Room							
Tax							
Restaurant							
Beverages							
Telephone - Local							
Telephone - L.D.							
Laundry							
Valet							
Misc. Charges							
Cash Disbursements							
Transfer Debits							
TOTAL DEBITS							
Cash Received							
Allowances							
Transfer to City Ledger							
Transfer Credit							
TOTAL CREDITS							
BALANCE FORWARD							

UNIVERSITY INN

Folio #: _____

Guest's Name: _____   Room #: _____

Departure Date: _____   Today's Date: _____

ALL ACCOUNTS ARE DUE WHEN RENDERED

DATE							
FORWARD							
Room							
Tax							
Restaurant							
Beverages							
Telephone - Local							
Telephone - L.D.							
Laundry							
Valet							
Misc. Charges							
Cash Disbursements							
Transfer Debits							
TOTAL DEBITS							
Cash Received							
Allowances							
Transfer to City Ledger							
Transfer Credit							
TOTAL CREDITS							
BALANCE FORWARD							

UNIVERSITY INN

Folio #: _____

Guest's Name: _____   Room #: _____

Departure Date: _____   Today's Date: _____

ALL ACCOUNTS ARE DUE WHEN RENDERED

DATE							
FORWARD							
Room							
Tax							
Restaurant							
Beverages							
Telephone - Local							
Telephone - L.D.							
Laundry							
Valet							
Misc. Charges							
Cash Disbursements							
Transfer Debits							
TOTAL DEBITS							
Cash Received							
Allowances							
Transfer to City Ledger							
Transfer Credit							
TOTAL CREDITS							
BALANCE FORWARD							

UNIVERSITY INN

Folio #: _____

Guest's Name: _____   Room #: _____

Departure Date: _____   Today's Date: _____

ALL ACCOUNTS ARE DUE WHEN RENDERED

DATE							
FORWARD							
Room							
Tax							
Restaurant							
Beverages							
Telephone - Local							
Telephone - L.D.							
Laundry							
Valet							
Misc. Charges							
Cash Disbursements							
Transfer Debits							
TOTAL DEBITS							
Cash Received							
Allowances							
Transfer to City Ledger							
Transfer Credit							
TOTAL CREDITS							
BALANCE FORWARD							

UNIVERSITY INN

Folio #: _____

Guest's Name: _____ Room #: _____

Departure Date: _____ Today's Date: _____

ALL ACCOUNTS ARE DUE WHEN RENDERED

DATE							
FORWARD							
Room							
Tax							
Restaurant							
Beverages							
Telephone - Local							
Telephone - L.D.							
Laundry							
Valet							
Misc. Charges							
Cash Disbursements							
Transfer Debits							
TOTAL DEBITS							
Cash Received							
Allowances							
Transfer to City Ledger							
Transfer Credit							
TOTAL CREDITS							
BALANCE FORWARD							

UNIVERSITY INN

Folio #: _____

Guest's Name: _____   Room #: _____

Departure Date: _____   Today's Date: _____

ALL ACCOUNTS ARE DUE WHEN RENDERED

DATE							
FORWARD							
Room							
Tax							
Restaurant							
Beverages							
Telephone - Local							
Telephone - L.D.							
Laundry							
Valet							
Misc. Charges							
Cash Disbursements							
Transfer Debits							
TOTAL DEBITS							
Cash Received							
Allowances							
Transfer to City Ledger							
Transfer Credit							
TOTAL CREDITS							
BALANCE FORWARD							

UNIVERSITY INN

Folio #: _____

Guest's Name: _____   Room #: _____

Departure Date: _____   Today's Date: _____

ALL ACCOUNTS ARE DUE WHEN RENDERED

DATE							
FORWARD							
Room							
Tax							
Restaurant							
Beverages							
Telephone - Local							
Telephone - L.D.							
Laundry							
Valet							
Misc. Charges							
Cash Disbursements							
Transfer Debits							
TOTAL DEBITS							
Cash Received							
Allowances							
Transfer to City Ledger							
Transfer Credit							
TOTAL CREDITS							
BALANCE FORWARD							

79

UNIVERSITY INN

Folio #: _____

Guest's Name: _____   Room #: _____

Departure Date: _____   Today's Date: _____

ALL ACCOUNTS ARE DUE WHEN RENDERED

DATE							
FORWARD							
Room							
Tax							
Restaurant							
Beverages							
Telephone - Local							
Telephone - L.D.							
Laundry							
Valet							
Misc. Charges							
Cash Disbursements							
Transfer Debits							
TOTAL DEBITS							
Cash Received							
Allowances							
Transfer to City Ledger							
Transfer Credit							
TOTAL CREDITS							
BALANCE FORWARD							

UNIVERSITY INN

Folio #: _____

Guest's Name: _____   Room #: _____

Departure Date: _____   Today's Date: _____

ALL ACCOUNTS ARE DUE WHEN RENDERED

DATE							
FORWARD							
Room							
Tax							
Restaurant							
Beverages							
Telephone - Local							
Telephone - L.D.							
Laundry							
Valet							
Misc. Charges							
Cash Disbursements							
Transfer Debits							
TOTAL DEBITS							
Cash Received							
Allowances							
Transfer to City Ledger							
Transfer Credit							
TOTAL CREDITS							
BALANCE FORWARD							

UNIVERSITY INN

Folio #: _____

Guest's Name: _____   Room #: _____

Departure Date: _____   Today's Date: _____

ALL ACCOUNTS ARE DUE WHEN RENDERED

DATE							
FORWARD							
Room							
Tax							
Restaurant							
Beverages							
Telephone - Local							
Telephone - L.D.							
Laundry							
Valet							
Misc. Charges							
Cash Disbursements							
Transfer Debits							
TOTAL DEBITS							
Cash Received							
Allowances							
Transfer to City Ledger							
Transfer Credit							
TOTAL CREDITS							
BALANCE FORWARD							

UNIVERSITY INN

Folio #: _____

Guest's Name: _____   Room #: _____

Departure Date: _____   Today's Date: _____

ALL ACCOUNTS ARE DUE WHEN RENDERED

DATE							
FORWARD							
Room							
Tax							
Restaurant							
Beverages							
Telephone - Local							
Telephone - L.D.							
Laundry							
Valet							
Misc. Charges							
Cash Disbursements							
Transfer Debits							
TOTAL DEBITS							
Cash Received							
Allowances							
Transfer to City Ledger							
Transfer Credit							
TOTAL CREDITS							
BALANCE FORWARD							

UNIVERSITY INN

Folio #: _____

Guest's Name: _____ Room #: _____

Departure Date: _____ Today's Date: _____

ALL ACCOUNTS ARE DUE WHEN RENDERED

DATE							
FORWARD							
Room							
Tax							
Restaurant							
Beverages							
Telephone - Local							
Telephone - L.D.							
Laundry							
Valet							
Misc. Charges							
Cash Disbursements							
Transfer Debits							
TOTAL DEBITS							
Cash Received							
Allowances							
Transfer to City Ledger							
Transfer Credit							
TOTAL CREDITS							
BALANCE FORWARD							

UNIVERSITY INN

Folio #: _____

Guest's Name: _____   Room #: _____

Departure Date: _____   Today's Date: _____

ALL ACCOUNTS ARE DUE WHEN RENDERED

DATE							
FORWARD							
Room							
Tax							
Restaurant							
Beverages							
Telephone - Local							
Telephone - L.D.							
Laundry							
Valet							
Misc. Charges							
Cash Disbursements							
Transfer Debits							
TOTAL DEBITS							
Cash Received							
Allowances							
Transfer to City Ledger							
Transfer Credit							
TOTAL CREDITS							
BALANCE FORWARD							

UNIVERSITY INN

Folio #: _____

Guest's Name: _____   Room #: _____

Departure Date: _____   Today's Date: _____

ALL ACCOUNTS ARE DUE WHEN RENDERED

DATE							
FORWARD							
Room							
Tax							
Restaurant							
Beverages							
Telephone - Local							
Telephone - L.D.							
Laundry							
Valet							
Misc. Charges							
Cash Disbursements							
Transfer Debits							
TOTAL DEBITS							
Cash Received							
Allowances							
Transfer to City Ledger							
Transfer Credit							
TOTAL CREDITS							
BALANCE FORWARD							

93

UNIVERSITY INN

Folio #: _____

Guest's Name: _____   Room #: _____

Departure Date: _____   Today's Date: _____

ALL ACCOUNTS ARE DUE WHEN RENDERED

DATE							
FORWARD							
Room							
Tax							
Restaurant							
Beverages							
Telephone - Local							
Telephone - L.D.							
Laundry							
Valet							
Misc. Charges							
Cash Disbursements							
Transfer Debits							
TOTAL DEBITS							
Cash Received							
Allowances							
Transfer to City Ledger							
Transfer Credit							
TOTAL CREDITS							
BALANCE FORWARD							

UNIVERSITY INN

Folio #: _____

Guest's Name: _____   Room #: _____

Departure Date: _____   Today's Date: _____

ALL ACCOUNTS ARE DUE WHEN RENDERED

DATE							
FORWARD							
Room							
Tax							
Restaurant							
Beverages							
Telephone - Local							
Telephone - L.D.							
Laundry							
Valet							
Misc. Charges							
Cash Disbursements							
Transfer Debits							
TOTAL DEBITS							
Cash Received							
Allowances							
Transfer to City Ledger							
Transfer Credit							
TOTAL CREDITS							
BALANCE FORWARD							

UNIVERSITY INN

Folio #: _____

Guest's Name: _____

Room #: _____

Departure Date: _____

Today's Date: _____

ALL ACCOUNTS ARE DUE WHEN RENDERED

DATE							
FORWARD							
Room							
Tax							
Restaurant							
Beverages							
Telephone - Local							
Telephone - L.D.							
Laundry							
Valet							
Misc. Charges							
Cash Disbursements							
Transfer Debits							
TOTAL DEBITS							
Cash Received							
Allowances							
Transfer to City Ledger							
Transfer Credit							
TOTAL CREDITS							
BALANCE FORWARD							

UNIVERSITY INN

Folio #: _____

Guest's Name: _____   Room #: _____

Departure Date: _____   Today's Date: _____

ALL ACCOUNTS ARE DUE WHEN RENDERED

DATE							
FORWARD							
Room							
Tax							
Restaurant							
Beverages							
Telephone - Local							
Telephone - L.D.							
Laundry							
Valet							
Misc. Charges							
Cash Disbursements							
Transfer Debits							
TOTAL DEBITS							
Cash Received							
Allowances							
Transfer to City Ledger							
Transfer Credit							
TOTAL CREDITS							
BALANCE FORWARD							

UNIVERSITY INN

Folio #: _____

Guest's Name: _____   Room #: _____

Departure Date: _____   Today's Date: _____

ALL ACCOUNTS ARE DUE WHEN RENDERED

DATE							
FORWARD							
Room							
Tax							
Restaurant							
Beverages							
Telephone - Local							
Telephone - L.D.							
Laundry							
Valet							
Misc. Charges							
Cash Disbursements							
Transfer Debits							
TOTAL DEBITS							
Cash Received							
Allowances							
Transfer to City Ledger							
Transfer Credit							
TOTAL CREDITS							
BALANCE FORWARD							

UNIVERSITY INN

Folio #: _____

Guest's Name: _____   Room #: _____

Departure Date: _____   Today's Date: _____

ALL ACCOUNTS ARE DUE WHEN RENDERED

DATE							
FORWARD							
Room							
Tax							
Restaurant							
Beverages							
Telephone - Local							
Telephone - L.D.							
Laundry							
Valet							
Misc. Charges							
Cash Disbursements							
Transfer Debits							
TOTAL DEBITS							
Cash Received							
Allowances							
Transfer to City Ledger							
Transfer Credit							
TOTAL CREDITS							
BALANCE FORWARD							

105

UNIVERSITY INN

Folio #: _____

Guest's Name: _____   Room #: _____

Departure Date: _____   Today's Date: _____

ALL ACCOUNTS ARE DUE WHEN RENDERED

DATE							
FORWARD							
Room							
Tax							
Restaurant							
Beverages							
Telephone - Local							
Telephone - L.D.							
Laundry							
Valet							
Misc. Charges							
Cash Disbursements							
Transfer Debits							
TOTAL DEBITS							
Cash Received							
Allowances							
Transfer to City Ledger							
Transfer Credit							
TOTAL CREDITS							
BALANCE FORWARD							

UNIVERSITY INN

Folio #: _____

Guest's Name: _____   Room #: _____

Departure Date: _____   Today's Date: _____

ALL ACCOUNTS ARE DUE WHEN RENDERED

DATE							
FORWARD							
Room							
Tax							
Restaurant							
Beverages							
Telephone - Local							
Telephone - L.D.							
Laundry							
Valet							
Misc. Charges							
Cash Disbursements							
Transfer Debits							
TOTAL DEBITS							
Cash Received							
Allowances							
Transfer to City Ledger							
Transfer Credit							
TOTAL CREDITS							
BALANCE FORWARD							

RESTAURANT DEPARTMENT CONTROL SHEET

NAME: _____   **DATE:** _____

VOUCHER #	ROOM NO.	GUEST NAME	AMOUNT	MEMO
			$	
		Total Amount	$	

BEVERAGE DEPARTMENT CONTROL SHEET

NAME: _____   **DATE:** _____

VOUCHER #	ROOM NO.	GUEST NAME	AMOUNT	MEMO
			$	
		Total Amount	$	

111

RESTAURANT DEPARTMENT CONTROL SHEET

NAME: _____ DATE: _____

VOUCHER #	ROOM NO.	GUEST NAME	AMOUNT	MEMO
			$	
		Total Amount	$	

BEVERAGE DEPARTMENT CONTROL SHEET

NAME: _____ DATE: _____

VOUCHER #	ROOM NO.	GUEST NAME	AMOUNT	MEMO
			$	
		Total Amount	$	

113

RESTAURANT DEPARTMENT CONTROL SHEET

NAME: _____   DATE: _____

VOUCHER #	ROOM NO.	GUEST NAME	AMOUNT	MEMO
			$	
		Total Amount	$	

BEVERAGE DEPARTMENT CONTROL SHEET

NAME: _____   DATE: _____

VOUCHER #	ROOM NO.	GUEST NAME	AMOUNT	MEMO
			$	
		Total Amount	$	

RESTAURANT DEPARTMENT CONTROL SHEET

NAME: _____   DATE: _____

VOUCHER #	ROOM NO.	GUEST NAME	AMOUNT	MEMO
			$	
		Total Amount	$	

BEVERAGE DEPARTMENT CONTROL SHEET

NAME: _____   DATE: _____

VOUCHER #	ROOM NO.	GUEST NAME	AMOUNT	MEMO
			$	
		Total Amount	$	

LONG DISTANCE TELEPHONE CONTROL SHEET

NAME: _____   DATE: _____

VOUCHER #	ROOM NO.	GUEST NAME	AMOUNT	MEMO
			$	
		Total Amount	$	

LOCAL TELEPHONE CONTROL SHEET

NAME: _____   DATE: _____

VOUCHER #	ROOM NO.	GUEST NAME	AMOUNT	MEMO
			$	
		Total Amount	$	

LONG DISTANCE TELEPHONE CONTROL SHEET

NAME: _____   **DATE:** _____

VOUCHER #	ROOM NO.	GUEST NAME	AMOUNT	MEMO
			$	
		Total Amount	$	

LOCAL TELEPHONE CONTROL SHEET

NAME: _____   **DATE:** _____

VOUCHER #	ROOM NO.	GUEST NAME	AMOUNT	MEMO
			$	
		Total Amount	$	

LONG DISTANCE TELEPHONE CONTROL SHEET

NAME: _____   DATE: _____

VOUCHER #	ROOM NO.	GUEST NAME	AMOUNT	MEMO
			$	
		Total Amount	$	

LOCAL TELEPHONE CONTROL SHEET

NAME: _____   DATE: _____

VOUCHER #	ROOM NO.	GUEST NAME	AMOUNT	MEMO
			$	
		Total Amount	$	

LONG DISTANCE TELEPHONE CONTROL SHEET

NAME: _____   DATE: _____

VOUCHER #	ROOM NO.	GUEST NAME	AMOUNT	MEMO
			$	
		Total Amount	$	

LOCAL TELEPHONE CONTROL SHEET

NAME: _____   DATE: _____

VOUCHER #	ROOM NO.	GUEST NAME	AMOUNT	MEMO
			$	
		Total Amount	$	

ALLOWANCE CONTROL SHEET

NAME: _____ DATE: _____

VOUCHER #	ROOM NO.	GUEST NAME	AMOUNT	MEMO
			$	
		Total Amount	$	

LAUNDRY DEPARTMENT CONTROL SHEET

NAME: _____ DATE: _____

VOUCHER #	ROOM NO.	GUEST NAME	AMOUNT	MEMO
			$	
		Total Amount	$	

ALLOWANCE CONTROL SHEET

NAME: _____   DATE: _____

VOUCHER #	ROOM NO.	GUEST NAME	AMOUNT	MEMO
			$	
		Total Amount	$	

LAUNDRY DEPARTMENT CONTROL SHEET

NAME: _____   DATE: _____

VOUCHER #	ROOM NO.	GUEST NAME	AMOUNT	MEMO
			$	
		Total Amount	$	

ALLOWANCE CONTROL SHEET

NAME: _____   DATE: _____

VOUCHER #	ROOM NO.	GUEST NAME	AMOUNT	MEMO
			$	
		Total Amount	$	

LAUNDRY DEPARTMENT CONTROL SHEET

NAME: _____   DATE: _____

VOUCHER #	ROOM NO.	GUEST NAME	AMOUNT	MEMO
			$	
		Total Amount	$	

131

ALLOWANCE CONTROL SHEET

NAME: _____   DATE: _____

VOUCHER #	ROOM NO.	GUEST NAME	AMOUNT	MEMO
			$	
		Total Amount	$	

LAUNDRY DEPARTMENT CONTROL SHEET

NAME: _____   DATE: _____

VOUCHER #	ROOM NO.	GUEST NAME	AMOUNT	MEMO
			$	
		Total Amount	$	

No. 1001

UNIVERSITY INN

Credit

Department

Date: _____ 19 ___

Name

Room or Acct. No.

Date	Symbol	Amount

Do not write in above space

EXPLANATION

Signed by: _____

Cut along double lines.

No. 1002

UNIVERSITY INN

Credit

Department

Date: _____ 19 ___

Name

Room or Acct. No.

Date	Symbol	Amount

Do not write in above space

EXPLANATION

Signed by: _____

Cut along double lines.

No. 1003

UNIVERSITY INN

Credit

Department

Date: _____ 19 ___

Name

Room or Acct. No.

Date	Symbol	Amount

Do not write in above space

EXPLANATION

Signed by: _____

No. 1004

UNIVERSITY INN

Credit

Department

Date: _____ 19 ___

Name

Room or Acct. No.

Date	Symbol	Amount

Do not write in above space

EXPLANATION

Signed by: _____

No. 1005

No. 1006

Credit

UNIVERSITY INN

Department

Date: _____ 19 ___

Name

Room or Acct. No.

Date	Symbol	Amount

Do not write in above space

EXPLANATION

Signed by: _____

Cut along double lines.

No. 1007

Credit

UNIVERSITY INN

Department

Date: _____ 19 ___

Name

Room or Acct. No.

Date	Symbol	Amount

Do not write in above space

EXPLANATION

Signed by: _____

Credit

UNIVERSITY INN

Department

Date: _____ 19 ___

Name

Room or Acct. No.

Date	Symbol	Amount

Do not write in above space

EXPLANATION

Signed by: _____

Cut along double lines.

No. 1008

Credit

UNIVERSITY INN

Department

Date: _____ 19 ___

Name

Room or Acct. No.

Date	Symbol	Amount

Do not write in above space

EXPLANATION

Signed by: _____

No. 1009

Credit

UNIVERSITY INN

Department _____

Date: _____ 19___

Name

Room or Acct. No. _____

Date	Symbol	Amount

Do not write in above space

EXPLANATION

Signed by: _____

Cut along double lines.

No. 1010

Credit

UNIVERSITY INN

Department _____

Date: _____ 19___

Name

Room or Acct. No. _____

Date	Symbol	Amount

Do not write in above space

EXPLANATION

Signed by: _____

Cut along double lines.

No. 1011

Credit

UNIVERSITY INN

Department _____

Date: _____ 19___

Name

Room or Acct. No. _____

Date	Symbol	Amount

Do not write in above space

EXPLANATION

Signed by: _____

No. 1012

Credit

UNIVERSITY INN

Department _____

Date: _____ 19___

Name

Room or Acct. No. _____

Date	Symbol	Amount

Do not write in above space

EXPLANATION

Signed by: _____

No. 1013

UNIVERSITY INN

Credit

Department ___

Name

Date: ___ 19___

Room or Acct. No.

Date	Symbol	Amount

Do not write in above space

EXPLANATION

Signed by: ___

Cut along double lines.

No. 1015

UNIVERSITY INN

Credit

Department ___

Name

Date: ___ 19___

Room or Acct. No.

Date	Symbol	Amount

Do not write in above space

EXPLANATION

Signed by: ___

No. 1014

UNIVERSITY INN

Credit

Department ___

Name

Date: ___ 19___

Room or Acct. No.

Date	Symbol	Amount

Do not write in above space

EXPLANATION

Signed by: ___

Cut along double lines.

No. 1016

UNIVERSITY INN

Credit

Department ___

Name

Date: ___ 19___

Room or Acct. No.

Date	Symbol	Amount

Do not write in above space

EXPLANATION

Signed by: ___

No. 1017

UNIVERSITY INN   **Credit**

Department

Date: _____ 19____

Name _____ Room or Acct. No.

Date	Symbol	Amount

Do not write in above space

EXPLANATION

Signed by: _____

Cut along double lines.

No. 1019

UNIVERSITY INN   **Credit**

Department

Date: _____ 19____

Name _____ Room or Acct. No.

Date	Symbol	Amount

Do not write in above space

EXPLANATION

Signed by: _____

No. 1018

UNIVERSITY INN   **Credit**

Department

Date: _____ 19____

Name _____ Room or Acct. No.

Date	Symbol	Amount

Do not write in above space

EXPLANATION

Signed by: _____

Cut along double lines.

No. 1020

UNIVERSITY INN   **Credit**

Department

Date: _____ 19____

Name _____ Room or Acct. No.

Date	Symbol	Amount

Do not write in above space

EXPLANATION

Signed by: _____

No. 1021

UNIVERSITY INN   **Credit**

Department

Date: 19

Name   Room or Acct. No.

Date   Symbol   Amount

Do not write in above space

EXPLANATION

Signed by:

Cut along double lines.

No. 1022

UNIVERSITY INN   **Credit**

Department

Date: 19

Name   Room or Acct. No.

Date   Symbol   Amount

Do not write in above space

EXPLANATION

Signed by:

Cut along double lines

No. 1023

UNIVERSITY INN   **Credit**

Department

Date: 19

Name   Room or Acct. No.

Date   Symbol   Amount

Do not write in above space

EXPLANATION

Signed by:

No. 1024

UNIVERSITY INN   **Credit**

Department

Date: 19

Name   Room or Acct. No.

Date   Symbol   Amount

Do not write in above space

EXPLANATION

Signed by:

145

No. 1025

UNIVERSITY INN

Department _____

Credit

Date: _____ 19 ___

Name _____   Room or Acct. No. _____

Date	Symbol	Amount

Do not write in above space

EXPLANATION

Signed by: _____

Cut along double lines.

No. 1027

UNIVERSITY INN

Department _____

Credit

Date: _____ 19 ___

Name _____   Room or Acct. No. _____

Date	Symbol	Amount

Do not write in above space

EXPLANATION

Signed by: _____

No. 1026

UNIVERSITY INN

Department _____

Credit

Date: _____ 19 ___

Name _____   Room or Acct. No. _____

Date	Symbol	Amount

Do not write in above space

EXPLANATION

Signed by: _____

Cut along double lines

No. 1028

UNIVERSITY INN

Department _____

Credit

Date: _____ 19 ___

Name _____   Room or Acct. No. _____

Date	Symbol	Amount

Do not write in above space

EXPLANATION

Signed by: _____

147

No. 1029

UNIVERSITY INN

Credit

Department _____

Date: _____ 19 __

Name _____

Room or Acct. No. _____

Date	Symbol	Amount

Do not write in above space

EXPLANATION

Signed by: _____

Cut along double lines.

No. 1030

UNIVERSITY INN

Credit

Department _____

Date: _____ 19 __

Name _____

Room or Acct. No. _____

Date	Symbol	Amount

Do not write in above space

EXPLANATION

Signed by: _____

Cut along double lines

No. 1031

UNIVERSITY INN

Credit

Department _____

Date: _____ 19 __

Name _____

Room or Acct. No. _____

Date	Symbol	Amount

Do not write in above space

EXPLANATION

Signed by: _____

No. 1032

UNIVERSITY INN

Credit

Department _____

Date: _____ 19 __

Name _____

Room or Acct. No. _____

Date	Symbol	Amount

Do not write in above space

EXPLANATION

Signed by: _____

No. 1033

Credit

UNIVERSITY INN

_____ Department

Name

Date: _____ 19____

Room or Acct. No. _____

Date	Symbol	Amount

Do not write in above space

EXPLANATION

Signed by: _____

Cut along double lines.

No. 1034

Credit

UNIVERSITY INN

_____ Department

Name

Date: _____ 19____

Room or Acct. No. _____

Date	Symbol	Amount

Do not write in above space

EXPLANATION

Signed by: _____

Cut along double lines

No. 1035

Credit

UNIVERSITY INN

_____ Department

Name

Date: _____ 19____

Room or Acct. No. _____

Date	Symbol	Amount

Do not write in above space

EXPLANATION

Signed by: _____

No. 1036

Credit

UNIVERSITY INN

_____ Department

Name

Date: _____ 19____

Room or Acct. No. _____

Date	Symbol	Amount

Do not write in above space

EXPLANATION

Signed by: _____

151

No. 1037

Credit

UNIVERSITY INN

_____ Department

Name

Date: _____ 19___

Room or Acct. No.

Date	Symbol	Amount

Do not write in above space

EXPLANATION

Signed by: _____

Cut along double lines.

No. 1039

Credit

UNIVERSITY INN

_____ Department

Name

Date: _____ 19___

Room or Acct. No.

Date	Symbol	Amount

Do not write in above space

EXPLANATION

Signed by: _____

No. 1038

Credit

UNIVERSITY INN

_____ Department

Name

Date: _____ 19___

Room or Acct. No.

Date	Symbol	Amount

Do not write in above space

EXPLANATION

Signed by: _____

Cut along double lines

No. 1040

Credit

UNIVERSITY INN

_____ Department

Name

Date: _____ 19___

Room or Acct. No.

Date	Symbol	Amount

Do not write in above space

EXPLANATION

Signed by: _____

153

No. 1041

UNIVERSITY INN

Credit

Department _____

Date: _____ 19__

Name _____

Room or Acct. No. _____

Date	Symbol	Amount

Do not write in above space

EXPLANATION

Signed by: _____

Cut along double lines.

No. 1043

UNIVERSITY INN

Credit

Department _____

Date: _____ 19__

Name _____

Room or Acct No. _____

Date	Symbol	Amount

Do not write in above space

EXPLANATION

Signed by: _____

No. 1042

UNIVERSITY INN

Credit

Department _____

Date: _____ 19__

Name _____

Room or Acct. No. _____

Date	Symbol	Amount

Do not write in above space

EXPLANATION

Signed by: _____

Cut along double lines

No. 1044

UNIVERSITY INN

Credit

Department _____

Date: _____ 19__

Name _____

Room or Acct. No. _____

Date	Symbol	Amount

Do not write in above space

EXPLANATION

Signed by: _____

155

No. 1045

UNIVERSITY INN
Credit

Department

Date: _____ 19

Name

Room or Acct. No.

Date	Symbol	Amount

Do not write in above space

EXPLANATION

Signed by:

Cut along double lines.

No. 1046

UNIVERSITY INN
Credit

Department

Date: _____ 19

Name

Room or Acct. No.

Date	Symbol	Amount

Do not write in above space

EXPLANATION

Signed by:

Cut along double lines

No. 1047

UNIVERSITY INN
Credit

Department

Date: _____ 19

Name

Room or Acct. No.

Date	Symbol	Amount

Do not write in above space

EXPLANATION

Signed by:

No. 1048

UNIVERSITY INN
Credit

Department

Date: _____ 19

Name

Room or Acct. No.

Date	Symbol	Amount

Do not write in above space

EXPLANATION

Signed by:

157

No. 1050

UNIVERSITY INN _____ Department

Credit

Name

Date: _____ 19

Room or Acct. No.

Date	Symbol	Amount

Do not write in above space

EXPLANATION

Signed by: _____

Cut along double lines

No. 1052

UNIVERSITY INN _____ Department

Credit

Name

Date: _____ 19

Room or Acct. No.

Date	Symbol	Amount

Do not write in above space

EXPLANATION

Signed by: _____

No. 1049

UNIVERSITY INN _____ Department

Credit

Name

Date: _____ 19

Room or Acct. No.

Date	Symbol	Amount

Do not write in above space

EXPLANATION

Signed by: _____

Cut along double lines.

No. 1051

UNIVERSITY INN _____ Department

Credit

Name

Date: _____ 19

Room or Acct. No.

Date	Symbol	Amount

Do not write in above space

EXPLANATION

Signed by: _____

No. 1053

UNIVERSITY INN

Credit

Department

Date: _____ 19___

Name

Room or Acct. No.

Date   Symbol   Amount

Do not write in above space

EXPLANATION

Signed by: _____

Cut along double lines.

No. 1054

UNIVERSITY INN

Credit

Department

Date: _____ 19___

Name

Room or Acct. No.

Date   Symbol   Amount

Do not write in above space

EXPLANATION

Signed by: _____

Cut along double lines

No. 1055

UNIVERSITY INN

Credit

Department

Date: _____ 19___

Name

Room or Acct. No.

Date   Symbol   Amount

Do not write in above space

EXPLANATION

Signed by: _____

No. 1056

UNIVERSITY INN

Credit

Department

Date: _____ 19___

Name

Room or Acct. No.

Date   Symbol   Amount

Do not write in above space

EXPLANATION

Signed by: _____

161

No. 1057

UNIVERSITY INN

Credit

Department _____

Date: _____ 19 ___

Name _____

Room or Acct. No. _____

Date	Symbol	Amount

Do not write in above space

EXPLANATION _____

Signed by: _____

Cut along double lines.

No. 1059

UNIVERSITY INN

Credit

Department _____

Date: _____ 19 ___

Name _____

Room or Acct. No. _____

Date	Symbol	Amount

Do not write in above space

EXPLANATION _____

Signed by: _____

No. 1058

UNIVERSITY INN

Credit

Department _____

Date: _____ 19 ___

Name _____

Room or Acct. No. _____

Date	Symbol	Amount

Do not write in above space

EXPLANATION _____

Signed by: _____

Cut along double lines

No. 1060

UNIVERSITY INN

Credit

Department _____

Date: _____ 19 ___

Name _____

Room or Acct. No. _____

Date	Symbol	Amount

Do not write in above space

EXPLANATION _____

Signed by: _____

163

Charge

UNIVERSITY INN

Department

Date: _____ 19___

Name

Room or Acct. No.

Date | Symbol | Amount

Do not write in above space

EXPLANATION

Signed by:

Cut along double lines.

No. 1003

Charge

UNIVERSITY INN

Department

Date: _____ 19___

Name

Room or Acct. No.

Date | Symbol | Amount

Do not write in above space

EXPLANATION

Signed by:

No. 1002

Charge

UNIVERSITY INN

Department

Date: _____ 19___

Name

Room or Acct. No.

Date | Symbol | Amount

Do not write in above space

EXPLANATION

Signed by:

Cut along double lines.

No. 1004

Charge

UNIVERSITY INN

Department

Date: _____ 19___

Name

Room or Acct. No.

Date | Symbol | Amount

Do not write in above space

EXPLANATION

Signed by:

No. 1005

UNIVERSITY INN

Charge

Department

Date: _____ 19___

Room or Acct. No.

Name

Date	Symbol	Amount

Do not write in above space

EXPLANATION

Signed by: _____

Cut along double lines.

No. 1007

UNIVERSITY INN

Charge

Department

Date: _____ 19___

Room or Acct. No.

Name

Date	Symbol	Amount

Do not write in above space

EXPLANATION

Signed by: _____

No. 1006

UNIVERSITY INN

Charge

Department

Date: _____ 19___

Room or Acct. No.

Name

Date	Symbol	Amount

Do not write in above space

EXPLANATION

Signed by: _____

Cut along double lines.

No. 1008

UNIVERSITY INN

Charge

Department

Date: _____ 19___

Room or Acct. No.

Name

Date	Symbol	Amount

Do not write in above space

EXPLANATION

Signed by: _____

No. 1009

Charge

UNIVERSITY INN

Department

Name

Date: _____ 19___

Room or Acct. No.

Date	Symbol	Amount

Do not write in above space

EXPLANATION

Signed by: _____

Cut along double lines.

No. 1011

Charge

UNIVERSITY INN

Department

Name

Date: _____ 19___

Room or Acct. No.

Date	Symbol	Amount

Do not write in above space

EXPLANATION

Signed by: _____

No. 1010

Charge

UNIVERSITY INN

Department

Name

Date: _____ 19___

Room or Acct. No.

Date	Symbol	Amount

Do not write in above space

EXPLANATION

Signed by: _____

Cut along double lines.

No. 1012

Charge

UNIVERSITY INN

Department

Name

Date: _____ 19___

Room or Acct. No.

Date	Symbol	Amount

Do not write in above space

EXPLANATION

Signed by: _____

169

No. 1013

UNIVERSITY INN

Charge

Department _____

Date: _____ 19 __

Name _____

Room or Acct. No. _____

Date	Symbol	Amount

Do not write in above space

EXPLANATION

Signed by: _____

Cut along double lines.

No. 1014

UNIVERSITY INN

Charge

Department _____

Date: _____ 19 __

Name _____

Room or Acct. No. _____

Date	Symbol	Amount

Do not write in above space

EXPLANATION

Signed by: _____

Cut along double lines.

No. 1015

UNIVERSITY INN

Charge

Department _____

Date: _____ 19 __

Name _____

Room or Acct. No. _____

Date	Symbol	Amount

Do not write in above space

EXPLANATION

Signed by: _____

No. 1016

UNIVERSITY INN

Charge

Department _____

Date: _____ 19 __

Name _____

Room or Acct. No. _____

Date	Symbol	Amount

Do not write in above space

EXPLANATION

Signed by: _____

No. 1017

UNIVERSITY INN

Charge

Department

Date: _____ 19 ___

Room or Acct. No.

Name

Date	Symbol	Amount

Do not write in above space

EXPLANATION

Signed by: _____

Cut along double lines.

No. 1019

UNIVERSITY INN

Charge

Department

Date: _____ 19 ___

Room or Acct No.

Name

Date	Symbol	Amount

Do not write in above space

EXPLANATION

Signed by: _____

No. 1018

UNIVERSITY INN

Charge

Department

Date: _____ 19 ___

Room or Acct. No.

Name

Date	Symbol	Amount

Do not write in above space

EXPLANATION

Signed by: _____

Cut along double lines.

No. 1020

UNIVERSITY INN

Charge

Department

Date: _____ 19 ___

Room or Acct. No.

Name

Date	Symbol	Amount

Do not write in above space

EXPLANATION

Signed by: _____

No. 1021

Charge

UNIVERSITY INN

Department _____

Name _____

Date: _____ 19

Room or Acct. No. _____

Date	Symbol	Amount

Do not write in above space

EXPLANATION _____

Signed by: _____

Cut along double lines.

No. 1023

Charge

UNIVERSITY INN

Department _____

Name _____

Date: _____ 19

Room or Acct. No. _____

Date	Symbol	Amount

Do not write in above space

EXPLANATION _____

Signed by: _____

No. 1022

Charge

UNIVERSITY INN

Department _____

Name _____

Date: _____ 19

Room or Acct. No. _____

Date	Symbol	Amount

Do not write in above space

EXPLANATION _____

Signed by: _____

Cut along double lines

No. 1024

Charge

UNIVERSITY INN

Department _____

Name _____

Date: _____ 19

Room or Acct. No. _____

Date	Symbol	Amount

Do not write in above space

EXPLANATION _____

Signed by: _____

175

No. 1025

UNIVERSITY INN

Charge

Department

Date: _____ 19___

Room or Acct. No.

Name

Date	Symbol	Amount

Do not write in above space

EXPLANATION

Signed by: _____

Cut along double lines.

No. 1027

UNIVERSITY INN

Charge

Department

Date: _____ 19___

Room or Acct No.

Name

Date	Symbol	Amount

Do not write in above space

EXPLANATION

Signed by: _____

No. 1026

UNIVERSITY INN

Charge

Department

Date: _____ 19___

Room or Acct. No.

Name

Date	Symbol	Amount

Do not write in above space

EXPLANATION

Signed by: _____

Cut along double lines

No. 1028

UNIVERSITY INN

Charge

Department

Date: _____ 19___

Room or Acct. No.

Name

Date	Symbol	Amount

Do not write in above space

EXPLANATION

Signed by: _____

No. 1029

UNIVERSITY INN

Charge

Department

Date: _____ 19___

Name _____

Room or Acct. No.

Date	Symbol	Amount

Do not write in above space

EXPLANATION

Signed by: _____

Cut along double lines.

No. 1031

UNIVERSITY INN

Charge

Department

Date: _____ 19___

Name _____

Room or Acct. No.

Date	Symbol	Amount

Do not write in above space

EXPLANATION

Signed by: _____

No. 1030

UNIVERSITY INN

Charge

Department

Date: _____ 19___

Name _____

Room or Acct. No.

Date	Symbol	Amount

Do not write in above space

EXPLANATION

Signed by: _____

Cut along double lines

No. 1032

UNIVERSITY INN

Charge

Department

Date: _____ 19___

Name _____

Room or Acct. No.

Date	Symbol	Amount

Do not write in above space

EXPLANATION

Signed by: _____

179

No. 1033

Charge

UNIVERSITY INN

Department _____

Date: _____ 19

Name _____

Room or Acct. No. _____

Date	Symbol	Amount

Do not write in above space

EXPLANATION _____

Signed by: _____

Cut along double lines.

No. 1035

Charge

UNIVERSITY INN

Department _____

Date: _____ 19

Name _____

Room or Acct. No. _____

Date	Symbol	Amount

Do not write in above space

EXPLANATION _____

Signed by: _____

No. 1034

Charge

UNIVERSITY INN

Department _____

Date: _____ 19

Name _____

Room or Acct. No. _____

Date	Symbol	Amount

Do not write in above space

EXPLANATION _____

Signed by: _____

Cut along double lines

No. 1036

Charge

UNIVERSITY INN

Department _____

Date: _____ 19

Name _____

Room or Acct. No. _____

Date	Symbol	Amount

Do not write in above space

EXPLANATION _____

Signed by: _____

No. 1037

Charge

UNIVERSITY INN

Department _____

Name _____

Date: _____ 19___

Room or Acct. No. _____

Date	Symbol	Amount

Do not write in above space

EXPLANATION

Signed by: _____

Cut along double lines.

No. 1038

Charge

UNIVERSITY INN

Department _____

Name _____

Date: _____ 19___

Room or Acct. No. _____

Date	Symbol	Amount

Do not write in above space

EXPLANATION

Signed by: _____

Cut along double lines

No. 1039

Charge

UNIVERSITY INN

Department _____

Name _____

Date: _____ 19___

Room or Acct. No. _____

Date	Symbol	Amount

Do not write in above space

EXPLANATION

Signed by: _____

No. 1040

Charge

UNIVERSITY INN

Department _____

Name _____

Date: _____ 19___

Room or Acct. No. _____

Date	Symbol	Amount

Do not write in above space

EXPLANATION

Signed by: _____

183

No. 1041

UNIVERSITY INN

Charge

_____ Department

Date: _____ 19___

Name _____ Room or Acct. No. _____

Date	Symbol	Amount

Do not write in above space

EXPLANATION _____

Signed by: _____

Cut along double lines.

No. 1042

UNIVERSITY INN

Charge

_____ Department

Date: _____ 19___

Name _____ Room or Acct. No. _____

Date	Symbol	Amount

Do not write in above space

EXPLANATION _____

Signed by: _____

Cut along double lines

No. 1043

UNIVERSITY INN

Charge

_____ Department

Date: _____ 19___

Name _____ Room or Acct. No. _____

Date	Symbol	Amount

Do not write in above space

EXPLANATION _____

Signed by: _____

No. 1044

UNIVERSITY INN

Charge

_____ Department

Date: _____ 19___

Name _____ Room or Acct. No. _____

Date	Symbol	Amount

Do not write in above space

EXPLANATION _____

Signed by: _____

185

No. 1045

Charge

UNIVERSITY INN

Department _____

Date: _____ 19 ___

Name _____

Room or Acct. No. _____

Date	Symbol	Amount

Do not write in above space

EXPLANATION

Signed by: _____

Cut along double lines.

No. 1047

Charge

UNIVERSITY INN

Department _____

Date: _____ 19 ___

Name _____

Room or Acct. No. _____

Date	Symbol	Amount

Do not write in above space

EXPLANATION

Signed by: _____

187

No. 1046

Charge

UNIVERSITY INN

Department _____

Date: _____ 19 ___

Name _____

Room or Acct. No. _____

Date	Symbol	Amount

Do not write in above space

EXPLANATION

Signed by: _____

Cut along double lines

No. 1048

Charge

UNIVERSITY INN

Department _____

Date: _____ 19 ___

Name _____

Room or Acct. No. _____

Date	Symbol	Amount

Do not write in above space

EXPLANATION

Signed by: _____

No. 1049

UNIVERSITY INN

Charge

Department _____

Date: _____ 19 ____

Name _____

Room or Acct. No. _____

Date	Symbol	Amount

Do not write in above space

EXPLANATION

Signed by: _____

Cut along double lines.

No. 1050

UNIVERSITY INN

Charge

Department _____

Date: _____ 19 ____

Name _____

Room or Acct. No. _____

Date	Symbol	Amount

Do not write in above space

EXPLANATION

Signed by: _____

Cut along double lines

No. 1051

UNIVERSITY INN

Charge

Department _____

Date: _____ 19 ____

Name _____

Room or Acct. No. _____

Date	Symbol	Amount

Do not write in above space

EXPLANATION

Signed by: _____

No. 1052

UNIVERSITY INN

Charge

Department _____

Date: _____ 19 ____

Name _____

Room or Acct. No. _____

Date	Symbol	Amount

Do not write in above space

EXPLANATION

Signed by: _____

No. 1053

No. 1054

Charge

_____ Department

UNIVERSITY INN

Date: _____ 19___

Name

Room or Acct. No.

Date	Symbol	Amount

Do not write in above space

EXPLANATION

Signed by: _____

Cut along double lines.

No. 1055

Charge

_____ Department

UNIVERSITY INN

Date: _____ 19___

Name

Room or Acct. No.

Date	Symbol	Amount

Do not write in above space

EXPLANATION

Signed by: _____

Charge

_____ Department

UNIVERSITY INN

Date: _____ 19___

Name

Room or Acct. No.

Date	Symbol	Amount

Do not write in above space

EXPLANATION

Signed by: _____

Cut along double lines

No. 1056

Charge

_____ Department

UNIVERSITY INN

Date: _____ 19___

Name

Room or Acct. No.

Date	Symbol	Amount

Do not write in above space

EXPLANATION

Signed by: _____

No. 1057

UNIVERSITY INN

Charge

_____ Department

Date: _____ 19____

Name _____

Room or Acct. No. _____

Date	Symbol	Amount

Do not write in above space

EXPLANATION

Signed by: _____

Cut along double lines.

No. 1058

UNIVERSITY INN

Charge

_____ Department

Date: _____ 19____

Name _____

Room or Acct. No. _____

Date	Symbol	Amount

Do not write in above space

EXPLANATION

Signed by: _____

Cut along double lines

No. 1059

UNIVERSITY INN

Charge

_____ Department

Date: _____ 19____

Name _____

Room or Acct. No. _____

Date	Symbol	Amount

Do not write in above space

EXPLANATION

Signed by: _____

No. 1060

UNIVERSITY INN

Charge

_____ Department

Date: _____ 19____

Name _____

Room or Acct. No. _____

Date	Symbol	Amount

Do not write in above space

EXPLANATION

Signed by: _____

UNIVERSITY INN
FRONT OFFICE CASH SHEET

Date:_____

Cash Receipts

Cash Disbursements - Guests

Room #	Name	Amount	Room #	Name	Item	Amount
			Guest Disbursements Subtotal			

Cash Disbursements - House

Room #	Name	Amount				
			House Disbursements Subtotal			

RECAPITULATION

			Total Receipts		
			Disbursements - Guests		
		+	Disbursements - House		
		-	Total Disbursements		
Cash Receipts Total		=	**Deposit**		

UNIVERSITY INN
FRONT OFFICE CASH SHEET

Date:_____

Cash Receipts · Cash Disbursements - Guests

Room #	Name	Amount	Room #	Name	Item	Amount
				Guest Disbursements Subtotal		

Cash Disbursements - House

House Disbursements Subtotal		

RECAPITULATION

	Total Receipts	
	Disbursements - Guests	
+	Disbursements - House	
-	Total Disbursements	
Cash Receipts Total	**= Deposit**	

197

UNIVERSITY INN
FRONT OFFICE CASH SHEET

Date:_____

Cash Receipts			Cash Disbursements - Guests			
Room #	Name	Amount	Room #	Name	Item	Amount
				Guest Disbursements Subtotal		
			Cash Disbursements - House			
			House Disbursements Subtotal			
			RECAPITULATION			
				Total Receipts		
				Disbursements - Guests		
			+	Disbursements - House		
			-	Total Disbursements		
	Cash Receipts Total		=	**Deposit**		

199

UNIVERSITY INN
FRONT OFFICE CASH SHEET

Date:_____

Cash Receipts			Cash Disbursements - Guests			
Room #	Name	Amount	Room #	Name	Item	Amount
				Guest Disbursements Subtotal		

Cash Disbursements - House

Room #	Name	Amount	Room #	Name	Item	Amount
				House Disbursements Subtotal		

RECAPITULATION

	Total Receipts	
	Disbursements - Guests	
+	Disbursements - House	
-	Total Disbursements	
Cash Receipts Total	**= Deposit**	

UNIVERSITY INN
FRONT OFFICE CASH SHEET

Date:_____

Cash Receipts			**Cash Disbursements - Guests**			
Room #	Name	Amount	Room #	Name	Item	Amount
				Guest Disbursements Subtotal		
			Cash Disbursements - House			
				House Disbursements Subtotal		
			RECAPITULATION			
				Total Receipts		
				Disbursements - Guests		
			+	Disbursements - House		
			-	Total Disbursements		
	Cash Receipts Total		=	**Deposit**		

UNIVERSITY INN
FRONT OFFICE CASH SHEET

Date:_____

Cash Receipts			**Cash Disbursements - Guests**			
Room #	Name	Amount	Room #	Name	Item	Amount
				Guest Disbursements Subtotal		
			Cash Disbursements - House			
			House Disbursements Subtotal			
			RECAPITULATION			
				Total Receipts		
				Disbursements - Guests		
			+	Disbursements - House		
			-	Total Disbursements		
Cash Receipts Total			**=**	**Deposit**		

UNIVERSITY INN
CLOSING BANK COUNT

Cashier Name:

Cashier Shift:

Date:

Bills:	$100.00	
	50.00	
	20.00	
	10.00	
	5.00	
	1.00	
Coins:	.50	
	.25	
	.10	
	.05	
	.01	
	Sub Total	
+	Due Back	
=	TOTAL BANK	

UNIVERSITY INN
CASH TURN-IN ENVELOPE

Cashier Name:

Cashier Shift:

Date:

Bills:	$100.00	
	50.00	
	20.00	
	10.00	
	5.00	
	1.00	
Coins:	.50	
	.25	
	.10	
	.05	
	.01	

Checks and Vouchers

Total Amount Enclosed	
- DUE BACK	
= DEPOSIT	
- DEPOSIT (from cash sheet)	
DIFFERENCE (over/short)	

UNIVERSITY INN
CLOSING BANK COUNT

Cashier Name:	
Cashier Shift:	
Date:	

Bills:	$100.00	
	50.00	
	20.00	
	10.00	
	5.00	
	1.00	
Coins:	.50	
	.25	
	.10	
	.05	
	.01	
	Sub Total	
+	Due Back	
=	**TOTAL BANK**	

UNIVERSITY INN
CASH TURN-IN ENVELOPE

Cashier Name:	
Cashier Shift:	
Date:	

Bills:	$100.00	
	50.00	
	20.00	
	10.00	
	5.00	
	1.00	
Coins:	.50	
	.25	
	.10	
	.05	
	.01	
Checks and Vouchers		
	Total Amount Enclosed	
	- DUE BACK	
	= DEPOSIT	
	- DEPOSIT (from cash sheet)	
	DIFFERENCE (over/short)	

UNIVERSITY INN
CLOSING BANK COUNT

Cashier Name:

Cashier Shift:

Date:

Bills:	$100.00
	50.00
	20.00
	10.00
	5.00
	1.00
Coins:	.50
	.25
	.10
	.05
	.01
	Sub Total
+	Due Back
=	TOTAL BANK

UNIVERSITY INN
CASH TURN-IN ENVELOPE

Cashier Name:

Cashier Shift:

Date:

Bills:	$100.00
	50.00
	20.00
	10.00
	5.00
	1.00
Coins:	.50
	.25
	.10
	.05
	.01

Checks and Vouchers

| Total Amount Enclosed |
| - DUE BACK |
| = DEPOSIT |
| - DEPOSIT (from cash sheet) |
| DIFFERENCE (over/short) |

UNIVERSITY INN
CLOSING BANK COUNT

Cashier Name:

Cashier Shift:

Date:

Bills:	$100.00	
	50.00	
	20.00	
	10.00	
	5.00	
	1.00	
Coins:	.50	
	.25	
	.10	
	.05	
	.01	
	Sub Total	
+	Due Back	
=	TOTAL BANK	

UNIVERSITY INN
CASH TURN-IN ENVELOPE

Cashier Name:

Cashier Shift:

Date:

Bills:	$100.00	
	50.00	
	20.00	
	10.00	
	5.00	
	1.00	
Coins:	.50	
	.25	
	.10	
	.05	
	.01	
Checks and Vouchers		
	Total Amount Enclosed	
	- DUE BACK	
	= DEPOSIT	
	- DEPOSIT (from cash sheet)	
	DIFFERENCE (over/short)	

213

UNIVERSITY INN
CLOSING BANK COUNT

Cashier Name:

Cashier Shift:

Date:

Bills:	$100.00		
	50.00		
	20.00		
	10.00		
	5.00		
	1.00		
Coins:	.50		
	.25		
	.10		
	.05		
	.01		
	Sub Total		
+	Due Back		
=	TOTAL BANK		

UNIVERSITY INN
CASH TURN-IN ENVELOPE

Cashier Name:

Cashier Shift:

Date:

Bills:	$100.00		
	50.00		
	20.00		
	10.00		
	5.00		
	1.00		
Coins:	.50		
	.25		
	.10		
	.05		
	.01		

Checks and Vouchers

Total Amount Enclosed		
- DUE BACK		
= DEPOSIT		
- DEPOSIT (from cash sheet)		
DIFFERENCE (over/short)		

215

UNIVERSITY INN
CLOSING BANK COUNT

Cashier Name:		
Cashier Shift:		
Date:		

Bills:	$100.00		
	50.00		
	20.00		
	10.00		
	5.00		
	1.00		
Coins:	.50		
	.25		
	.10		
	.05		
	.01		
	Sub Total		
+	Due Back		
=	TOTAL BANK		

UNIVERSITY INN
CASH TURN-IN ENVELOPE

Cashier Name:		
Cashier Shift:		
Date:		

Bills:	$100.00		
	50.00		
	20.00		
	10.00		
	5.00		
	1.00		
Coins:	.50		
	.25		
	.10		
	.05		
	.01		
Checks and Vouchers			
	Total Amount Enclosed		
-	DUE BACK		
=	DEPOSIT		
-	DEPOSIT (from cash sheet)		
	DIFFERENCE (over/short)		

217

UNIVERSITY INN
ROOM AND HOUSE COUNT SHEET

Date: _____

Room Reconciliation

	No. of Rooms	No. of Persons	Room Value		Tax Value
Yesterday					
+ Arrivals					
= Total					
- Departures					
= **Today**					

Room Statistics

Rooms Available	
Rooms Occupied	
House Count	
Average Rate per Occupied Room	$
Average Rate per Guest	$
Percentage of Occupancy	%
Average Number of Guests per Room	

Usually prepared from room rack.

Room #	No. of Guests	Tax	Room Rate
201			
202			
203			
204			
205			
206			
207			
208			
209			
210			
TOTAL			

UNIVERSITY INN
ROOM AND HOUSE COUNT SHEET

Date: _____

Usually prepared from room rack.

Room #	No. of Guests	Tax	Room Rate
201			
202			
203			
204			
205			
206			
207			
208			
209			
210			
TOTAL			

Room Reconciliation

	No. of Rooms	No. of Persons	Room Value	Tax Value
Yesterday				
+ Arrivals				
= Total				
- Departures				
= Today				

Room Statistics

Rooms Available	
Rooms Occupied	
House Count	
Average Rate per Occupied Room	$
Average Rate per Guest	$
Percentage of Occupancy	%
Average Number of Guests per Room	

UNIVERSITY INN
ROOM AND HOUSE COUNT SHEET

Date: _____

Room Reconciliation

	No. of Rooms	No. of Persons	Room Value	Tax Value
Yesterday				
+ Arrivals				
= Total				
- Departures				
= Today				

Room Statistics

Rooms Available	
Rooms Occupied	
House Count	
Average Rate per Occupied Room	$
Average Rate per Guest	$
Percentage of Occupancy	%
Average Number of Guests per Room	

Usually prepared from room rack.

Room #	No. of Guests	Tax	Room Rate
201			
202			
203			
204			
205			
206			
207			
208			
209			
210			
TOTAL			

UNIVERSITY INN
ROOM AND HOUSE COUNT SHEET

Date: _____

Usually prepared from room rack.

Room #	No. of Guests	Tax	Room Rate
201			
202			
203			
204			
205			
206			
207			
208			
209			
210			
TOTAL			

Room Reconciliation

	No. of Rooms	No. of Persons	Room Value	Tax Value
Yesterday				
+ Arrivals				
= Total				
- Departures				
= Today				

Room Statistics

Rooms Available	
Rooms Occupied	
House Count	
Average Rate per Occupied Room	$
Average Rate per Guest	$
Percentage of Occupancy	%
Average Number of Guests per Room	

225

UNIVERSITY INN
ROOM AND HOUSE COUNT SHEET

Date: _____

Room Reconciliation

	No. of Rooms	No. of Persons	Room Value	Tax Value
Yesterday				
+ Arrivals				
= Total				
- Departures				
= Today				

Room Statistics

Rooms Available	
Rooms Occupied	
House Count	
Average Rate per Occupied Room	$
Average Rate per Guest	$
Percentage of Occupancy	%
Average Number of Guests per Room	

Usually prepared from room rack.

Room #	No. of Guests	Tax	Room Rate
201			
202			
203			
204			
205			
206			
207			
208			
209			
210			
TOTAL			

UNIVERSITY INN
ROOM AND HOUSE COUNT SHEET

Date: _____

Room Reconciliation

	No. of Rooms	No. of Persons	Room Value	Tax Value
Yesterday				
+ Arrivals				
= Total				
- Departures				
= Today				

Room Statistics

Rooms Available	
Rooms Occupied	
House Count	
Average Rate per Occupied Room	$
Average Rate per Guest	$
Percentage of Occupancy	%
Average Number of Guests per Room	

Usually prepared from room rack.

Room #	No. of Guests	Tax	Room Rate
201			
202			
203			
204			
205			
206			
207			
208			
209			
210			
TOTAL			

University Inn
Daily Transcript of Guest Ledger

1	2	3	4	5	6	7	8	9	10	11	12	13	14	15	16	17	18	19	20	21	22
Folio No.	Room No.	No. of Guests	Opening Balance DB (CR)	Room	Room Tax	Restau- rant	Bever- ages	Local Calls	Long Distance	Laun- dry	Valet	Misc. Charge	Cash Disburse.	Transfer Debit	Total Daily Charges	Cash Receipts	Allow- ances	Transfer to City Ledger	Transfer Credit	Total Credits	Closing Balance

Sub Total

DEPARTURES

Sub Total

GRAND TOTAL

HOUSE

231

University Inn
Daily Transcript of Guest Ledger

1	2	3	4	5	6	7	8	9	10	11	12	13	14	15	16	17	18	19	20	21	22
Folio No.	Room No.	No. of Guests	Opening Balance DB (CR)	Room	Room Tax	Restau- rant	Bever- ages	Local Calls	Long Distance	Laun- dry	Valet	Misc. Charge	Cash Disburse.	Transfer Debit	Total Daily Charges	Cash Receipts	Allow- ances	Transfer to City Ledger	Transfer Credit	Total Credits	Closing Balance

Sub Total

DEPARTURES

Sub Total

GRAND TOTAL HOUSE

University Inn
Daily Transcript of Guest Ledger

1	2	3	4	5	6	7	8	9	10	11	12	13	14	15	16	17	18	19	20	21	22
Folio No.	Room No.	No. of Guests	Opening Balance DB (CR)	Room	Room Tax	Restau-rant	Bever-ages	Local Calls	Long Distance	Laun-dry	Valet	Misc. Charge	Cash Disburse.	Transfer Debit	Total Daily Charges	Cash Receipts	Allow-ances	Transfer to City Ledger	Transfer Credit	Total Credits	Closing Balance
Sub Total																					
DEPARTURES																					
Sub Total																					
GRAND TOTAL																					
HOUSE																					

University Inn
Daily Transcript of Guest Ledger

1	2	3	4	5	6	7	8	9	10	11	12	13	14	15	16	17	18	19	20	21	22
Folio No.	Room No.	No. of Guests	Opening Balance DB (CR)	Room	Room Tax	Restau- rant	Bever- ages	Local Calls	Long Distance	Laun- dry	Valet	Misc. Charge	Cash Disburse.	Transfer Debit	Total Daily Charges	Cash Receipts	Allow- ances	Transfer to City Ledger	Transfer Credit	Total Credits	Closing Balance
Sub Total																					
DEPARTURES																					
Sub Total																					
GRAND TOTAL																					
HOUSE																					

University Inn
Daily Transcript of Guest Ledger

1	2	3	4	5	6	7	8	9	10	11	12	13	14	15	16	17	18	19	20	21	22
Folio No.	Room No.	No. of Guests	Opening Balance DB (CR)	Room	Room Tax	Restau- rant	Bever- ages	Local Calls	Long Distance	Laun- dry	Valet	Misc. Charge	Cash Disburse.	Transfer Debit	Total Daily Charges	Cash Receipts	Allow- ances	Transfer to City Ledger	Transfer Credit	Total Credits	Closing Balance
Sub Total																					
DEPARTURES																					
Sub Total																					
GRAND TOTAL																					
HOUSE																					

239

University Inn
Daily Transcript of Guest Ledger

1	2	3	4	5	6	7	8	9	10	11	12	13	14	15	16	17	18	19	20	21	22
Folio No.	Room No.	No. of Guests	Opening Balance DB (CR)	Room	Room Tax	Restau- rant	Bever- ages	Local Calls	Long Distance	Laun- dry	Valet	Misc. Charge	Cash Disburse.	Transfer Debit	Total Daily Charges	Cash Receipts	Allow- ances	Transfer to City Ledger	Transfer Credit	Total Credits	Closing Balance
Sub Total																					

DEPARTURES

Sub Total																					

| GRAND TOTAL HOUSE | | | | | | | | | | | | | | | | | | | | | |

InnSyst - Front Desk Simulation

Instructions and Exercise

The following sections of InnSyst will illustrate the "manual" concepts you have worked through in the first part of this workbook in a "computer" environment. As you do the problem in InnSyst, try to understand the increased accuracy and decreased number of steps necessary compared to the manual system.

Section 1

Introduction

The InnSyst Front Desk Simulation software was designed to be used as a front desk demonstration program, allowing the student to process a fictitious day's transactions, which are included in the exercise portion of this manual. This program functions very much like a "real" front desk system. Unlike most fully functional systems however, this simulation is portable. It may be used on most computers **other than** original IBM PC's that used 320 or 360K diskettes. Thus, students may run the simulation in most labs or in their own rooms. Features of the simulation include the ability to process reservations, check-in guests, post charges, view a guest's balance, and check a guest out. In addition, the program will automatically perform the night audit function of posting room and tax, and balancing the night audit. The student is responsible for running the various reports and turning them in upon completing the assignment.

This manual is to assist students in using the software. It includes optional hard disk installation instructions and expanded directions for using the various functions. Also included are system requirements and system configuration options. (See the section in the night audit for changing the printer set-up.)

System Requirements

The minimum software and hardware requirements to run the Front Desk Simulation are:

√ The software comes on a 3 ½" disk. It will run on a 5 1/4" high density disk (not old style 360K diskettes) as well.

√ The software will run on an IBM PC, AT or compatible. A hard disk with **1** megabyte (free) is **highly** recommended. (Processing on diskettes is very slow; the processor must retrieve data at the transfer rate of the diskette).

√ An EGA or VGA monitor is recommended.

√ Microsoft or PC DOS operating system, version 2.1 (3.1 or later recommended).

√ A printer for printing the end of day reports.

Section 2

Installation and Start-up

No special installation is required. The program may be run directly from the diskette, however installation on a hard disk is recommended, because the software will run very slowly on diskettes. If installing on a hard disk, follow the following instructions. Otherwise, skip this section and proceed to start-up.

Hard Disk Installation

To install the software on a hard disk do the following:

1.   Insert your diskette in drive A.

2.   From drive A, Type "Finstall". The installation program will ask you to install the software on drive C in a directory called Fdesk. Press enter to accept.

3.   You will be asked three questions -- do you wish to install the programs, copy data, and do you want to update your configuration file. Answer yes to all three questions.

4.   When the copying is done you will be advised that the installation is done. That's all there is to it! Whenever entering the program, you will have to start-up your computer, and change directories whenever entering the program. This is done by typing CD\FDESK. At the completion of the exercise (and after turning in the project), you may remove the software by:

Removing Software from Hard Disk

1.   Erasing the software. From C:\Fdesk> Type **Erase *.***   . The operating system will ask you if you are sure. Respond by entering a "y", and the information will be erased.

2.   You may then remove the directory. From C:> type **RD Fdesk**.

Start-Up and Initialization

The software program starts by simply typing "hotel". The method will be slightly different depending upon the drive that your are using. If working from drive A, at the DOS prompt A > type **Hotel** and enter. If you followed the recommendation, and installed the software on a hard drive, you must first type (from C>) **CD\Fdesk**, and then **Hotel** and enter. On first access, you will be presented with an initialization screen, like the one that follows. Subsequently, it will not appear.

Figure 2.1: Initialization Screen

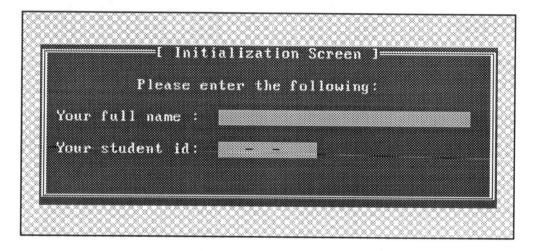

The initialization screen is shown in Figure 2.1. Your are asked to supply your full name, and your student ID. This information is used to personalize your copy, and also will print at the bottom of your reports. If you make a mistake, you may correct entry errors by using the cursor keys. Make sure the information is correct. Respond with a "Y" when asked to accept data. If it is not correct, respond to the prompt with "N", or anything other than "y". **You cannot change this later**.

246

Section 3

The Front Office Exercise

Introduction

In this section, students are required to check-out guests (who are already in the hotel), post charges and credits, perform the night audit functions, and print all reports. These indicate that the project was completed. These transactions will occur on **11/14/95**. There are fifteen transactions that must be completed followed by the posting of several charges, which are listed as transaction sixteen. To complete the exercise, post room and tax charges, print all reports, and determine the cash deposit and variance.

Exercise

Front Desk Transactions (11/14/95):

1. Mr. Michael Brown checked out of room 202 after incurring a breakfast charge. Mr. Brown paid in cash. (Post the charges that follow first)!

2. Theater tickets arrived for Larry Evans in room 201. Mr. Evans had authorized the paid-out in the amount of $25.00.

3. It was discovered that Mr. Ray Welsher in room 208 had left without paying his bill. Check-out the room by transferring the balance to the City Ledger.

4. Ms. Gail Anderson, who holds a reservation, has arrived, and must be checked in. Assign her to room 205.

5. Mr. Jacobs, of room 209, has authorized a miscellaneous charge of $20.00 for typing done by the hotel.

6. Mr. Rudy Heats checked out of room 210, by paying with his American Express card.

7. Mr. Kyle Bryant, who holds a reservation, has arrived. Check him into room 206. Mr. Bryant paid for three nights in advance (room and tax), with a check. **The room tax rate is 10% of the room rate.**

8. Mr. & Mrs. Robert Espe, and daughter, April, who hold a reservation, have arrived. Assign them to room 202.

9. Ms. Leta Durreta checked out of room 203 (POST HER CHARGES FIRST!). She paid for her charges by using her VISA credit card.

10. Mr. Dave Butker checks out of room 204, (after all his charges have been posted.) He paid by Diner's Club.

11. Mr. Henry Winker, who holds a reservation, has arrived. Check him in to the suite, room 210.

12. Mr. Tony Farras has arrived, and requests a room. (He doesn't have a reservation.) Check him in to room 208. His address is 1400 Dallas Parkway, Dallas, Texas 75258. Phone: (214) 334 - 6000. He is alone, his room type is a "D", the rate is $50.00, and he pays in advance for two nights room and tax.

13. Mr. Ron Redford and Mr. Charles McGruff have arrived, and request a room. (They do not have a reservation.) They will share a room and request separate bills. They both work for Hyers Hotels at 14000 Palmer Ln, Chicago, IL 60230. Phone: (312) 655 - 4000. Assign them to room 204, type "E". The full rate is $60.00 and each will pay half. They will stay one night.

14. A restaurant charge of $10.00 was posted to Mr. Jacobs (room 209) today by mistake. The charge should be posted to Mr. Farras (room 208). Correct the error on room 209 and re-post the charge on room 208.

15. The G.M. just informed you that Mr. Evans in Room 201 is a V.I.P. from GTPDN, Inc. Mr. Evans was supposed to be complimentary last night. An adjustment must be processed in the amount of $46.20 ($42.00 Room and $4.20 Tax).

16. The following charges must be posted:

Restaurant Summary November 14, 1995			Beverage Summary November 14, 1995		
202	Brown	$4.75	204	Redford	$14.25
207	Nielsen	$11.88	210	Winker	$57.00
203	Durreta	$9.50	209	Jacobs	$28.50
204	Butker	$4.99	208	Farras	$23.75
209	Jacobs	$16.15	201	Evans	$76.00
206	Bryant	$5.70	204	McGruff	$23.75
205	Anderson	$3.80			
207	Nielson	$47.50			
210	Winker	$85.50			
208	Farras	$10.00			

Long Distance Telephone Summary November 14, 1995			Local Telephone Summary November 14, 1995		
203	Durreta	$6.46	203	Durreta	$1.00
204	Butker	$8.55	204	Butker	$0.50
210	Winker	$47.50	209	Jacobs	$0.50
209	Jacobs	$4.28	210	Winker	$3.50
204	McGruff	$9.03			
207	Nielsen	$4.75			
205	Anderson	$7.60			

Laundry Summary November 14, 1995		
201	Evans	$11.88
208	Farras	$14.25
210	Winker	$71.25
205	Anderson	$7.13
206	Bryant	$7.60

Room charges must be posted by calling the room charges option from the night audit pull-down menu. Room charges are automatically posted. Room tax is 10% of the room rate and is also automatically posted.

Reports

The final step in the night audit is to produce the various daily reports. Print each report in turn and verify that the night audit is in balance. The only report that will require some manual effort is the cash report. You must calculate the overage or shortage by count and make a deposit. Assume that after counting all monies on hand, you have $835.92 comprised of the following:

Cash on hand: The following are the contents of the cash drawer at the close of business.

Personal Checks:
Mr. Kyle Bryant		$165.00
Mr. Tony Farras		$110.00
Bills:	$20.00	$200.00
	$10.00	$100.00
	$5.00	$150.00
	$1.00	$65.00
Rolled Coins:	.25	$30.00
	.10	$5.00
	.05	$4.00
	.01	$.50
Loose Coins:	.25	$3.50
	.10	$1.40
	.05	$1.00
	.01	$.52

The drawer started with a $500.00 bank.

Using the Cash Report, calculate the cash variance. List your deposit and your ending bank separately by type of currency. Use the format listed previously in this workbook.

Section 4

The Front Desk Main Menu

Figure 4.1: The Front Desk Main Menu

Figure 4.1 shows the front desk main menu that appears after the initialization has been completed. The main menu is a horizontal bar menu with pull-down menus attached. The functions available at the main menu are "Front Desk", "Night Audit", "Reports" and "Quit". To access any of these functions, simply move the cursor over to the desired area and press the enter key. The pop-up menu will appear with the choices available. If you made a mistake in pop-up selection, use the escape key, which will erase the pop-up.

You may use the letter "Q" to quit the program. After exiting or quitting the program, you will be returned to the DOS prompt. Never turn off the computer without exiting a program first.

If you installed the software on a hard disk, you will have to compete the project in one sitting, unless you copy all files in the directory back to your original diskette. Consult your DOS manual to do this. If you run the program from the diskette, you do not have to complete a project from beginning to end at one sitting. (However, the exercise is not lengthy and can be accomplished in one sitting.) Each time you exit any function your work will be automatically saved. Thus, if you complete part of the project and want to take a break, exit the program and return to it later. It is not a good idea to leave a computer program running. Open data files are subject to corruption due to any number of causes. Therefore, it is recommended that you quit and return by restarting (typing "hotel"), if you desire a break. When returning to the project, start with the transactions that you haven't done. The computer will accept duplicating entries, but this will put incorrect balances on your folios.

Section 5

Front Desk Operations

The front desk options include the eight choices shown in the pull-down menu in figure 4 - 1 and a new function "Correct Credits". The others are "Check-in", "Post charges", "Post credits", "View folio", "Edit Guest", "Change Rooms", "Late Charges" and "Check-out".

A. Check-in

Check-in procedures vary depending upon whether the arriving guest has a reservation or not. If not, the guest is said to be a walk-in. Thus, when the check-in option is chosen, the program will first ask if this guest is a walk-in or a reservation. The correct response is "R" for reservation or "W" for walk-in.

Figure 5.1: Registration Entry Screen

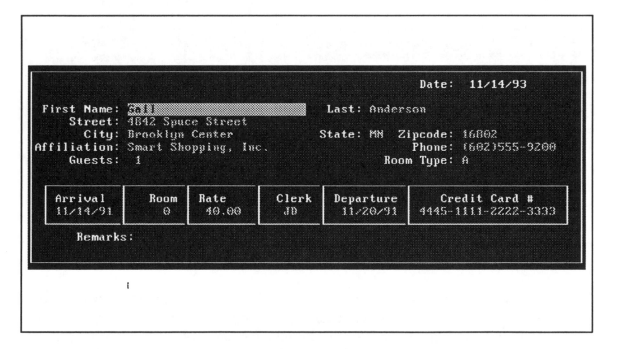

The data entry screen for walk-ins and reservations is the same (see Figure 5.1), but there is an additional step involved in the reservation process. Since reservation data is already on hand, the information is supplied to the registration form by the reservation file. This is done by the use of a pick list. The pick list is simply a screen that allows you to select the guest at check-in. When the pick list appears, select the desired record and enter. The registration form will be completed from the information stored in the reservation record. Thus, it is not necessary to complete all the information from a reservation. What is required, is to complete the bottom portion of the registration card. Depress the return key as necessary to get to the arrival date.

252

Date - Change to today (11/14/95) and enter.

Arrival date - Input the Operations date (11/14/95). The system will not accept an invalid date.

Room - select the room number that has been chosen for the guest. If it is unknown, the "F10" key may be used to check for available rooms. The program will not allow an invalid room number. **Selecting a room number of zero will cancel the operation.**

Rate - input the rate (i.e. 50) and enter.

Clerk - Put in your initials.

Departure - Input the departure date - (the slashes are not necessary).

After all the information is entered, the program will ask if it is okay to accept this check-in. Respond "Y", or "N". Note that if the room number is zero, it will not be added.

In the case of walk-ins, the registration card screen will be identical, but all information must be entered. Essentially, this means that the personal information must be completed, as supplied in the exercise. In addition, the room type must be chosen.

Room types - Valid room types are A - H. Other types will not be accepted. In fact, an invalid type will produce a pop-up screen with the valid choices shown, as in the reservation model. Place a letter in this field. (No return is necessary.)

The remainder of this data screen is completed as in the check-in for a reservation. See the above section.

B.   Charge Posting

Charge posting includes recording sales on a guest account. These sales may take the form of room sales, room tax, restaurant charges, bar charges, local and long distance charges, guest laundry charges, paid-outs, or miscellaneous sales. These charge accounts have all been given a code, which must be entered when posting the charges. The procedure is as follows. First, select the charge posting option from the front desk pull-down menu. A pick list will be provided of the guest in house, (and for those already checked out). Note that all charges should be posted before check-out; however, this program allows for that oversight.

Figure 5.2: Charge Posting Screen

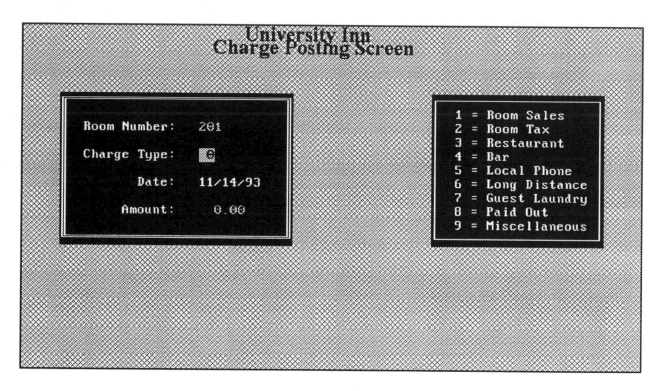

Once the guest is selected, the charge posting screen (figure 5.2) will be displayed. Since the guest has already been chosen, the room number will be already displayed. Follow the directions for the other fields as follows:

Charge type   Select from the choices at the screen at the right. (i.e., the restaurant charge code is 3) An invalid code will not be accepted.

Date   The date must be the operations date (11/14/95) change it and enter.

Amount   Enter the amount of the charge as shown on the department charge sheets given in the exercise instructions.

In the event of an error, the cursor keys may be used to backup. However, after the amount field has been entered, the program will ask if it is okay to accept the charge. Respond "Y" , after reviewing the charge, or "N" to reject it. **Important point to remember:** after the charge has been entered and posted, it cannot be removed. If a charge was incorrectly entered, use a correction to reverse it.

Finally, the program will ask if you wish to enter more charges. Respond "Y" or "N" and enter. If the response is "Y", the process will repeat. If "N", the program will terminate, post the transactions and return to the main menu.

C.   Credit Posting

The procedure for credit posting is identical to charge posting. Credits consist of advance deposits, corrections and adjustments. (Corrections are to correct today's errors, adjustments are to correct prior day's errors and/or are to record rebates to guests.) Codes have been assigned to advance deposits, corrections and adjustments and they are displayed along with the credit posting screen.

Credits are posted by selecting the credit posting option from the front desk pull-down menu. After hitting the enter key, a pick list will appear from which to select the guest that the credit must be posted to. Once the guest has been chosen, the credit posting screen will appear and the room number field will be displayed. The other entry fields must be completed as follows:

Charge type   Choose a valid type from the three choices displayed at the right. Other choices will not be accepted.

Date   Use the operations date (11/14/95).

Amount   Enter the amount as provided in the instructions to the exercise.

After completing the amount field, a prompt will ask if it is okay to post the credit. The correct response is "Y" or "N" and enter. A "Y" (yes) will record the transaction; a "N" will ignore it. Another prompt will ask if any more transactions are to be posted. Respond "Y" or "N". If "Y", the program will start the process over; "N" will post the charges and return to the main menu. **Important point to remember:** if a credit was posted in error, it cannot be undone. Correct it by entering a negative correction or a miscellaneous charge.

D.   Edit Guest

This section is used to correct errors made upon check in. A pick list is displayed similar to those shown in earlier sections. Once selected, a guest's record may be edited with the exception of two fields. These fields are the guest's last name and the room number. These are primary index fields and require additional handling. The last name cannot be changed. The room number can be changed, but that activity is a room change and is properly handled using the "Change Room" Function that follows. Once a guest is selected from a pick list, the registration information can be amended as needed.

E.   Correct Credits

This function is new and is used to fix errors that students make (and that commonly occur in practice). Credits include adjustment entries and all forms of settlements. Thus, if a payment was incorrectly recorded and discovered, this function can be used to correct the entry, after which the correct amount (if any) should be re-posted. Credits to be corrected include cash, adjustments, the credit card settlement accounts and the city ledger account. The screen looks and acts like that for the "Post Charges" and "Post Credit" screens.

F.   Change Rooms

This section is used for the necessity of changing a guest's room number. Presumably this will occur if a guest is not satisfied with his or her room, desires an upgrade, or is joined by another guest. Room changes usually require a change in room rate as well. Hence the program will display the usual pick list, the old room number and request the new room number and rate. Note that if the rate is left blank (zero), the guest's rate will become zero.

G.   View Folio

Selection of this option from the front desk pull-down will enable the viewer to see the posted details of a guest's folio. This is useful to verify that transactions were posted or simply to see the status of an account. In addition, a guest may wish to see his or her bill before paying it. Assuming that the front desk PC monitor is on a swivel, this option would enable a guest to view his or her charges without having to have a printout.

After selecting this option from the pull-down, a pick list will appear from which to select the guest 's account. A folio showing all charges and credits will be displayed. The bottom of the screen will prompt "Press any key when finished viewing." Press any key to return to the main menu.

H. Check-out

The check-out process selects the guest to check out from a pick list and then displays that guest's folio. The clerk enter the check-out payment code and the guest is checked out. This process occurs as follows:

1. Select the check-out option from the front desk pull-down menu.

2. Choose the guest and room number from the pick list that is displayed, by moving the cursor to the desired guest and enter.

3. A screen like that shown in figure V-8 will be displayed. It will ask for the payment code. Enter zero and a pop up screen will provide the appropriate codes for Cash, AMEX, etc. The program will not accept an invalid code.

4. Press any key to continue and enter the number of the code (31-35). **Do not** press enter. This will respond to the prompt "Okay to check-out?" with a no response.

5. After the code is accepted, you will be asked if it is okay to check this guest out. Respond "Y" or "N" as appropriate. A "N" response will abort the check-out. "Y" will proceed with the check-out and return to the main menu.

I. Late Charges

In the instance of a charge occurring after the guest has checked out, a late charge posting is necessary. In this instance, the charge may be posted by using the late charge function. The function does two things. First, the guest is checked back in and a charge transaction entry is automatically recorded. When this function is called, a pick list is displayed showing the checked out guests. Once selected, the program will ask if it is okay to re-check in this guest. Respond "Y" or "N" as necessary. If the response is yes, you will be taken into the transaction processing screen. Note that since the guest has been checked in again, it will be necessary to check him or her out again.

Section 6

Night Audit and Utilities

A hotel night auditor in a computerized property is often responsible for many tasks that are not part of the night audit balancing process. Some of these duties are incorporated in the pull-down options of the night audit pull-down. The selections available are "Room Charges", "Re-Index Files" and "End of Day".

A.   Room Charges

Room charges in a computer night audit is essentially a one-button process. From the Night Audit pull-down menu select the Room Charges option and enter. The room & tax process will begin. A message will say that process is underway. At the completion, the main menu will re-appear. The program looks in the room master file and posts the room rate in the file to each guest's folio in turn and updates all balances. In a larger property this process may take some time. In addition, room tax of 10% is automatically added to each folio.

As a safeguard, room & tax cannot be posted more than once each day. Thus, care should be taken to do this process only after all guests have been checked-in. It is a good idea to perform a back-up of the data files before invoking this function. Data files are particularly subject to corruption whenever a lengthily process is underway. Any power surge can permanently damage these files. In addition, since the room charge function cannot be undone, a back-up is highly recommended. Back-up may be accomplished by making a copy of all .DBF files and .NTX files using the DOS copy command.

B.   Re-index Files

Re-indexing files is a utility function that should be done each night by the night auditor. Data base files have indexes that point to the data in the files. They help in making searches speedy for either guest look-ups, like folio searches or for printing reports. Indexes, like data files, are subject to damage, particularly if any power surges occur. It is recommended that this function be done before any reports are printed.

This process is very simple. Simply select the Re-index option from the night audit pull-down menu. Messages will advise that this process is underway and the main menu will return upon completion. Since the hotel database is small, the process should not take longer than one minute and much less on a fast PC.

C.   End of Day

The end of day procedure is the last thing the night auditor does. Care must be taken that this is the last thing! In fact, a flashing warning box will ask for confirmation, before this process proceeds. This is because this process Zaps (erases) all transactions for the day. Once this is done, transaction reports may no longer be printed. It also gets rid of the checked-out guests, changes the date and allows room charges to be posted again. Therefore, this process should be done only with care. If in doubt, don't do it! It is essential to preparing for a new day. In other words, if an additional day is to be processed, this step is required. If not, the process is optional.

Section 7

Reports

The report pull-down, provides a selection of the various reports needed for the front office program. The various choices and their respective purposes are:

1. Transactions - to print the day's transactions by charge type.

2. Ledger - to print the balances in the account, listed by room number.

3. D Card - to print the night audit summary and daily sales.

4. Cash Report - prints the total cash received and paid-out.

5. Statistics - shows the occupancy and average rate statistics for the day.

The process for printing reports is fairly self-evident. Simply choose the desired report from the Report pull-down and press enter. A message will print asking you to wait - some of the reports require extensive sorting and calculations before printing. When this process is completed, a message will say that the report is printing. At the completion of the printing, the program will return to the main menu.

Review the reports after they are printed. Specifically, the following should be noted for each.

1. **Transactions:** Are all of the transactions from the exercise included? If not, the transaction was not entered. If room and tax are not included, the room posting process was not completed. Correct the situation and run the report again.

2. **Ledger:** The ledger report total balance must agree to the "Ending Balance" on the D Card report. If this is not the case, there is a problem with the database. The only possible fix is to re-index the files and try printing the report again. If this doesn't solve the problem, notify your instructor.

3. **D Card:** This report should show all sales for the day and balance to the total ledger. If it doesn't, try re-indexing the data files and print the report again. If it still doesn't work, notify your instructor.

4. **Cash Report:** This report lists the total cash taken in and the total paid-out. It is used as a basis for making the day's deposit. (The net cash is the amount that is supposed to be deposited.) Any variance will be the difference between the amount on hand (after subtracting the starting bank) and the net cash.

5.   **Statistics:** This report shows the number of rooms occupied, the number of guests, the average rate, occupancy percentage and the room sales per guest. It is used to track these statistics for the day and is updated on a daily basis, then added to the monthly data.

InnSyst Sample Reports

Sample reports from InnSyst can be found on the following pages. Each report is used in the night audit process to verify room rates, charges, credits and balances. The reports include the transaction report, the ledger report, the D Card report, room statistics and daily cash report.

University Inn
Transaction Report for 11/14/95

Code	Description	Room	Amount
3	**Restaurant**		
	Jacobs	209	<u>10.00</u>
Total			10.00
4	**Bar**		
	Evans	201	<u>100.00</u>
Total			100.00
5	**Local Phone**		
	Evans	201	1.00
	Evans	201	<u>2.00</u>
Total			3.00
8	**Paid-out**		
	Welsher	208	<u>25.00</u>
Total			25.00
31	**Cash**		
	Evans	201	<u>100.00</u>
Total			100.00
32	**MC-Visa**		
	Butker	204	118.50
	Evans	201	<u>3.00</u>
Total			121.50
Total Transactions			<u>359.50</u>

263

University Inn
Ledger Report for 11/14/95

Room	Description	Date	Charges	Credits	Balance
202	Brown				
	Room Sales	11/13/95	60.00		
	Room Tax	11/13/95	6.00		
	Restaurant	11/13/95	12.50		
	Local Phone	11/13/95	.50		
	Long Distance	11/13/95	4.75		
					83.75**
204	Butker				
	Room Sales	11/13/95	60.00		
	Room Tax	11/13/95	6.00		
	Restaurant	11/13/95	20.00		
	Beverage	11/13/95	12.50		
	Paid-out	11/13/95	20.00		
	M/C-Visa	11/14/95		118.50	
					0.00**
203	Durreta				
	Room Sales	11/13/95	45.00		
	Room Tax	11/13/95	4.50		
	Restaurant	11/13/95	12.50		
	Beverage	11/13/95	20.00		
	Local Phone	11/13/95	.50		
	Laundry	11/13/95	7.50		
	Cash	11/13/95		50.00	
					40.00**

University Inn
D Card Report for 11/14/95

Description	Amount
Rooms Sales	0.00
Room Tax	0.00
Restaurant	10.00
Beverage	100.00
Local Phone	3.00
Long Distance	0.00
Laundry	0.00
Paid-out	25.00
Miscellaneous	0.00
Total Debits	138.00

Adjustments	0.00
Cash	100.00
M/C - Visa	118.50
AMEX	0.00
C/B - Diners	0.00
City Ledger	0.00
Total Credits	218.50

Net Total -80.50

Opening Balance 894.15

Ending Balance 813.65

University Inn
Statistics Report for 11/14/95

Room	Guest Name	Room Rate	# of Guests
201	Evans	0.00	2
202	Brown	60.00	3
202	King	0.00	1
203	Durreta	45.00	2
207	Nielson	42.00	1
208	Welsher	50.00	2
209	Jacobs	40.00	1
210	Heats	120.00	2
	Totals	357.00	14

Summary Statistics

Occupied Rooms	7
Occupied - Paid Rooms	6
Occupancy Percentage	70.0%
Room Sales	357.00
Average Daily Rate	$ 59.50
Room Sales Per Guest	$ 25.50

University Inn
Daily Cash Report for 11/14/95

Description	**Amount**

Cash Received

Evans	100.00
Total Cash Received	100.00

Cash Paid-out

Welsher	25.00
Total Cash Paid-out	25.00

Net Cash	75.00

Deposit Worksheet

Opening Cash	500.00
Plus: Turn In (Above)	_____
Equals Calculated Cash on Hand	_____
Less: Actual Cash Count	_____
Equals: Over or (Short)	_____

University Inn
Daily Transcript of Guest Ledger

1	2	3	4	5	6	7	8	9	10	11	12	13	14	15	16	17	18	19	20	21	22
Folio No.	Room No.	No. of Guests	Opening Balance DB (CR)	Room	Room Tax	Restaurant	Beverages	Local Calls	Long Distance	Laundry	Valet	Misc. Charge	Cash Disburse.	Transfer Debit	Total Daily Charges	Cash Receipts	Allowances	Transfer to City Ledger	Transfer Credit	Total Credits	Closing Balance
Sub Total																					
DEPARTURES																					
Sub Total																					
GRAND TOTAL HOUSE																					

269

University Inn
Daily Transcript of Guest Ledger

	1	2	3	4	5	6	7	8	9	10	11	12	13	14	15	16	17	18	19	20	21	22
	Folio No.	Room No.	No. of Guests	Opening Balance DB (CR)	Room	Room Tax	Restau- rant	Bever- ages	Local Calls	Long Distance	Laun- dry	Valet	Misc. Charge	Cash Disburse.	Transfer Debit	Total Daily Charges	Cash Receipts	Allow- ances	Transfer to City Ledger	Transfer Credit	Total Credits	Closing Balance
Sub Total																						
DEPARTURES																						
Sub Total																						
GRAND TOTAL HOUSE																						

Notes

Notes

Notes

Notes